LEMON

LEMON

Marni Leigh Greenwald

ISBN 978-0-578-49520-0

Cover Photo Credit: Marni Leigh Greenwald

Printed in the United States of America

www.marnileigh.com

Cover and Interior Design: Creative Publishing Book Design

To Sierra—
My beautiful child, whose capacities are limitless.
Butterfly kisses.

To all those who are faced with something
that seems insurmountable;
There are jagged edges. There are smoother surfaces.
Today we walk with courage.

With love,
Marni

Author's Intent

The author's intent is to bring awareness about childhood illnesses and diagnoses. Lemon is a mother's quest for understanding the underlying medical conditions of her child. It is her courage and determination in discovering the most effective approaches and techniques; including support from doctors, therapists, and teachers to create an optimal environment for her child to thrive, and to ultimately heal from within.

The Moment

I sat frozen, still for a moment. Situated on the semi-soft black leather wooden bench in my dining room, slightly hunched over a blank screen. The warmth of the sun cascading through the window caressed my heart. In between the tree branches emitted a light, an opening signaling the birth of a new day. Blue skies overhead.

It was snowing outside. The beauty held within the intricacies of each snowflake reminded me of the unique qualities found within us all. Gracefully, they fell. Streams of wintry cool air flowed through the crevices of my window panes, as the whistling from the gusts of winds whirled about. As I circled my finger about the crusty piece of toast, I imagined elements of my life merging together in a symphonic like fashion. Harmony aligned with rhythm. In between the chords sounded key elements that evoked a softer quality found in the strumming of the strings; it created a song so eloquent. Accompanying this was a VOICE I longed to hear.

I puckered my lips tightly. My tongue pressed firmly upon my palette. It was as if I could taste the words as they emanated through me, up towards my diaphragm, through my larynx, and into the opening of my voice box. An old educational show from the seventies, "Electric Company" came to mind. The profile of two silhouettes faced one another. Their mouths adjacent, as they exhaled sounds, slowly with effortless ease. These formed interlocking prefixes and suffixes of singular words. Just as they blew a set of unified sounds, new one's were emerging. Softly, I rested my cheek against my palm.

I ventured deeper into a place where the receptive quality from mother nature's bounties became expressive on its own terms. Walking towards the ocean, my feet parlayed into sultry white sands. As I reached the shoreline, I watched the waves gallantly adjoin into one another. Within its calm surrender, in these crystalline waters, I saw my reflection.

I wiggled my feet out from beneath me and gently placed them on the floor. I had a plush backyard trimmed with a variety of oak, maple, and evergreen trees. A lovely, warm home. I turned up the heat from my living room with a cup o' coffee laden with cream. Like the solvent to a solution about to unfold, I took but a sip of it.

An Unconditional Love

Bundled in my chic-soft, nylon-polyester scarf wearing one of my favorite cotton t-shirts—a staple in my collection, one might surmise I was comfortable. One might even suggest a perk of being a "stay at home" mom. Though my days at home seemed long overdue, I had a purpose for being here. Here, in this place for a very significant reason.

As my fingers tapped the keys across a snow colored screen, I heard the pitter-pattering of my Jack Russell's lowly white paws. Briskly, she walked towards me. I shifted my gaze upon her. Her expressive dark chocolate brown eyes peered up at me with an undying loyalty and unwavering tenacity. I asked, "Do you want a bone?" Magnolia Louise, who we referred to as "Maggie", tilted her sweet little head. I tilted my head right back at her in a congenial way. I dashed into the kitchen adjacent to the dining room I reclined in. I turned the corner where I opened the narrow doorway of the pantry. Before my hand was in the box, Maggie sat eagerly, wagging her paintbrush-like tail. As I swiveled my body around, she swiftly took hold of the bone. She darted into the living room and dropped it on the bamboo rug. Rubbing her scent all over it, she had marked her territory. In all her glory, Maggie gave a little snort. Then, ravished it in an instant.

Dogs: They brought out the best in us, an unconditional love. Maggie's larger than life personality emanated from her small, muscular fifteen-pound body. If I were lucky enough, I'd look up at her at just the right time as she smiled and proudly showed me her "teethies". There were no words; a reminder of the simple things.

Time

It was time to unravel the ties hidden behind a taciturn curtain of disbelief. Physically tired and emotionally drained, something compelled me, something nudged at me to share these thoughts-the ones that ruminated my mind on a daily basis, the ones that touched me in ways that through the hardships invoked a powerful surge from within me.

I reached into the pockets of my youth where a shiny gold key appeared. I unlocked a door that led me to a place where I entered into the highest agreement with myself. In a vulnerable space, I aspired to have an insurmountable courage. This was the antecedent in transforming a beyond difficult experience into a more positive one.

My shoulders tensed up. Pangs of doubt ran through me. Surely, I had written stories before. One I published titled, "What Kind of Bagel am I?" Lighthearted and whimsical, it contained analogies about what types of personalities preferred certain flavored bagels. This one was more intimate and hit much closer to home.

My father's low tone, soft spoken voice swept through me; "Marni—You are like two years behind." It was as if I needed to be in a rush to get to the finish line. He was dissatisfied in my reluctance to enrolling in a master's program, yet concerned about my future, wanting me to be more independent. Yet, I was the ripe old age of twenty-four back then.

I was accepted into graduate school that year for a master's degree in Creative Arts Therapy. I enrolled in two classes, a six-credit class in counseling and a three-credit class in creative arts therapy. I was apprehensive about whether to continue my degree in art therapy, counseling, or marriage and family therapy. My college professor from my counseling class agreed to meet with me. She summed up from our brief meeting, "Not making a decision is making a decision."

It was in stark juxtaposition to that of my father's words. Even though, my teacher had a background in counseling, my father had a greater impact upon me. I agonized about whether to change my major, as I was concerned about opportunities in the field with a population I enjoyed. Working with children with multiple challenges and with health-related issues, I was passionate about. Empathy and creativity were at the forefront. These were the inherent qualities that made a profound difference in this world. Little did I know this was preparing me for something much more personal in my life.

Spirituality

I was drawn towards those who were evolved spiritually, the enlightened ones—Mother Theresa, Dalai Lama, and those who had an endless amount of compassion who led by the greatest principals-To serve others, honoring one's heart with authenticity, and speaking from the deepest parts of one's soul.

It was essential that I continued uncovering the more delicately woven layers. I reminded myself of the power of intention. I had the power, the ability, and the knowledge. I was inclined to pick up some reading material from the past. Books I indulged in, in my quest for understanding the more deeply rooted aspects of the self. As I went downstairs to my musty smelling basement, I was drawn to a box that read "Books*" on it. I unfolded the top in anticipation. I found a thick biblical type of blue book called, "A Course in Miracles". I grabbed an old raggedy blanket and sat in the corner as I opened it. The passages evoked something powerful—To live in a way that consisted of brevity with faith, and an undying love. It was written by Helen Schucman and her channeling the Voice of God. Marianne Williamson, a spiritual teacher, lecturer, and activist-taught, "A Course in Miracles" for over thirty years. I enjoyed her book, "A Return to Love: Reflections on the Principles of a Course in Miracles. I had the fortunate opportunity to attend a speaking engagement she was at. It resonated with a deeper part of me, in the collective consciousness of my heart and soul.

As if a little bird tapped me on the shoulder, I was reminded to face life boldly with belief in God, the angels, and myself. Admittedly, I didn't always have the answers. I was allowed to make mistakes. I would give myself permission as a sacred contract within myself to let go, and ultimately forgive.

A Manual for Self-Growth

I came across a thick white manual that read "Kripalu". As I opened it, there were depictions of various yogic postures with their Sanskrit names. I turned to a page that contained material about the four classes I led in the small group I was assigned to. It was all in practice to become a yoga teacher. At twenty-six years of age, I had enrolled in a month-long intensive yoga certification training program. It was held at a spiritual retreat at Kripalu in Lenox, Massachusetts. People from many different backgrounds, cultures, and nationalities had attended and that spanned the ages of eighteen to sixty years old. Powerful mantras throughout the classes assisted me in awakening to my wiser, more evolved self. These enlightened thoughts became integrated into my mind, body, and spirit. In each incremental movement there was a cause and effect reaction, allowing for greater healing. As I held these postures for longer periods, I breathed in fluidly, and awakened to a place of heightened awareness. It was as if I placed my finger on pause. Through the practice of yoga which signified union, a greater sense of harmony could be found in the solidification of thyself. Therefore, a more fulfilling life could be received with equanimity and with grace. I realigned composites of my body within a sphere of influence where the synaptic channels provided a release of that which did not serve me. It reached further into other processes within our systems, into the smallest units encompassing the cells. This served as the potential for unlimited healing.

Nearing the end of the program, I realized the powerful impact it had on me, as I assimilated so much valuable information. One thing that I was drawn to was as part of this transformational experience, was painting. I was inspired to create an art mural, though with the classes' participation. When I shared with the instructors, they responded favorably to this idea. During my two and a half hour drive home, I recalled being more in touch with my environment-the subtleties of the birds chirping, the trees swaying, and the beauty in the array and the variety of flowers. The chatter quieted, and the smog lifted, as I entered into a more peaceable place.

I arrived at my childhood home. I had been temporarily living there, as it was a transitional time and a turning point for me during my late twenties. I gathered up my juicy tempera paints, packed up my car, and resumed the space I was in. When I returned to the retreat, I was excited to begin this process with my fellow yogis. They joined with me in the cafeteria, a more spacious room. This was more conducive for an art mural.

As I continued reading my manual, I found the entry that contained my meditation. I invited the class to close their eyes and imagine when they first arrived here at the center—To simply, let go, breathing in and out, becoming more aware of the subtleties happening within their bodies, and greater in touch with their senses; to explore the time where they first arrived at the retreat. Perhaps, it was the touch of someone's hand, an experience or smell of that which was inviting, the sound of silence or laughter, or whatever it may be. There was a long pause. Then, when they were ready, I encouraged them to open their eyes. The paints were carefully, placed in front of them to draw upon their reflections.

I invited my yogi friends to close their eyes, again becoming aware of whatever sensations arose, and any thoughts that came up throughout their stay. Then, opening their eyes, again and painting whatever images they saw. Lastly, closing their eyes once more, to anything that may have arisen upon leaving. Upon opening them, they were invited to create anything that assisted them in their completion of a journey at the center.

The tangible representation of presenting this through a fluid medium offered a way to experience a cathartic release and a greater understanding of one's self. As one relaxed into a more forgiving state gathering information from the beginning, middle, and end, an assimilation of the whole of these parts could be bridged. A more cohesive sense of self could manifest, as we allowed our innate impulses and drives to be touched upon. A continuity in the sharing of this experience was welcomed.

The Current

Every decision I made mattered. Whatever I chose to partake in had a direct impact upon me, and therefore another. As I set my sights on the horizon, the dividing line became more transparent. It was essential that I face the more arduous moments. If I ignored or denied them, they would present themselves, even more intensely. As I stepped out of my comfort zone, I gave myself the opportunity for self-growth and expansion.

I peered out my windowsill through the box like structures on the panes. The skyline comforted me with cobalt blues, indigo purples, and viridian green hues. The light submerged through the shadows, and I felt part of a larger sphere of existence. The dendrites held within me, as in the extension of my fingers would be utilized. Graciously, I would use my hands to express an artistry, undefined. I gave power to my voice, upon the keys I touched. The output of viable words on the screen inspired me. The big picture. The white slate I could draw upon. The vacancy was all mine.

The undertones of crimson reds, vermillion oranges and royal yellow hues ignited like a placid fire within me. I watched them dispersing into open air. Like a Jackson Pollack painting, in between the chaos, my story unfolded. I carried the colors. My brush at hand.

Motherhood—
The Greatest Gift

At the ripe old age of thirty-nine, my parents visited in celebration of my birthday. It was July 11, 2009. As my parents neared the entryway of our charming cottage like home, I could not believe my eyes. It was my dollhouse from when I was a little girl. I could still smell the wood, as if it were just yesterday. Dad built it with some help from my sister and me. I had been about seven years old. Recently, I thought of it, and was inclined to ask my parents about it. I walked upstairs with my dad to our second bedroom. Just as he placed it on the floor, I noticed the seventies like interior. After all these years, it still contained the shag rugs, the small wicker and wooden furniture, and many of the tiny accessories. I looked into the little girl's bedroom, all pink and frilly. It struck me as something pivotal that was missing from my life.

Six weeks later, I took a pregnancy test that revealed a positive result. Within four months of receiving acupuncture from a dedicated acupuncturist who specialized in fertility, I had become pregnant. It was one of those things, I believed would just happen. A small miracle, larger than life. On July 10, 2009, I was blessed with this beautiful soul. The day after that, my parents had brought my old doll house over, and wouldn't you know it, I had already been pregnant.

So much I ruminated upon, concerning motherhood. Was I prepared enough? I reminded myself of the experiences I had with children. At fourteen years old, during my summer's off from school, I held jobs in day camps being a counselor for young girls. Throughout college, I took courses in child development and interned at day care centers. Later, I decided on a career path majoring in elementary education. I received my teaching degree and returned to college to take classes in special education. I took the leap of faith to bridge art with psychology and continued on to receive my master's degree in art therapy. I worked with medically ill children as well as children with multiple challenges. This was the foundation for my preparation in becoming a mother.

Forwards or backwards, it was still mom; a name that would remain with me for the rest of my life. My manual for entering this treatise of motherhood meant gathering as much information as I could including breastfeeding, duration of sleep, appropriate developmental milestones, and other health related issues. I attended a weekly birthing class that was ongoing for six weeks. In addition, I enrolled in a spiritual dance-movement workshop for pregnant mothers. I found it to be a very soulful and uplifting experience. We sat in a circle, meditating, reflecting, and exploring all aspects of ourselves drawing upon our own innate power. Then, we created a piece of art.

I held positive thoughts with daily mantras; "Appreciate the moment", "Listen to your heart's intent", "Blossom in your light", "Stand in your power", "Breathe in purity, exhale waste". I reaffirmed there was a beautiful spirit growing inside of me, and how sacred an experience this was. Although I felt compelled to go to my mother for support during this critical time, I hadn't wanted to cause her any additional worry. Ideally, I would have loved her to be with me throughout my labor, however I knew that wasn't going to be an option. Mom didn't want to see me in pain. She would be at the hospital, which I greatly appreciated.

My husband Andy would be by my side. Loyal, responsible and kind-I could always count on him. He still opened doors for me, cooked meals for us, helped out with laundry and with everyday life. Often, Andy put my needs and interests before his, whether we went to a particular restaurant, attended an event, etc. When it came to expressing emotions, that proved to be more difficult for him. On our second date, he confided to me that he wasn't very spiritual. I believed in miracles, not merely being coincidences.

As we continued our relationship, he professed to me that I opened him up to a place where he believed in things not always seen but felt, and that it wasn't always circumstantial. I was happy for him, as I knew life could be challenging. Believing in a higher power was helpful. In addition, I was more inclined to adhere to a philosophy which held a qualitative process which could evolve into being more quantitative in thought. Still, the finer qualities held within us supported one another. We found stability in each other's strengths, especially in some of the tougher times.

Turning Inwards, Towards the Womb

I closed my eyes, as I reached down and placed my hands upon my rounded belly. I was amazed at how this tiny seed was growing inside of me. I sat in my living room, legs outstretched, feet outwards, up on my ottoman. I listened to a variety of soft mellow folk music, while I took out some delicious soft pastels. I drew a silhouette from the neck down to just below the belly. It was a depiction of a mother with a baby growing in the womb. A series of these drawings, I continued throughout the next few months. It proved to be very cathartic.

Her sacredness held within my womb, she entrusted me with. Without television and an I-Pad in there, it was a quieter and gentler environment. She bathed in the richness of amniotic fluid. I would do everything in my power to create a warm environment for her, to provide a safe place for her during the day, and to rest her head. Each day that passed was closer to the moment; I would welcome her into my arms. I aspired to be a positive role model for her and foster a profound strength in her. It was essential that she followed her heart, trusted her instincts, and had the courage to live out her dreams. In the simplest of ways, my wish for her was to become exactly who she was, and to never, ever give up on herself.

Being respected as an artist, as a profession was challenging. However, earning an income came secondary to its more altruistic meaning, for my desire to paint, apply pastels, pencils, or any type of pen or ink, and put my ideas onto a tangible surface, pulsed through me. It was as fluid as drinking water. When women in the business world put on their high heeled shoes, suits, or more sophisticated dresses, I was dressing down. I preferred a colorful shirt with jeans or something black, maybe adding a splash of color with a hat, some fun jewelry, comfy sneakers, or boots. I was always trying to find that balance between what l was drawn to, and what I had to do. It was something I would continue exploring, as a soon to be mother.

What's in a Name

As the weeks passed, questions arose from family and friends. The most frequently asked question was, "What would her name be?" I had a few of the latest baby books given to me from my entrusted friend, Lori. Like a sister; I knew her since my early college days. She was genuine, kind, and joyous despite hardships. She listened without judgment, which was a very important quality. Upon selecting a name for our child, she believed that the right name would present, itself.

My grandmother, Sarah had passed a few years, prior to my pregnancy. Small in stature, yet you could hear her loud tone of voice emanating from the other room. She was my "Nanny", so very special. As a little girl she referred to me as "buby" (short for "bubula", meaning sweet heart; dear) and pinched my cheeks, just as I arrived and prior to me leaving. She loved my "Papa" Lenny (kind of like a mild version of Archie Bunker having a good heart) playing mahjong, walking to the avenue, attending the pool during the summer, and showing off her grandchildren. They lived modestly, in a small apt in Bayside-Queens, NY.

It was essential for me to have a family heritage name. Immediately I thought of my Nanny. It was on my radar to have as the first letter an, "S". The name-Sierra came to me. I searched for its meaning online. Sierra; the jagged edge of a mountain. The first time I said her name aloud, I felt a kick within me. "Hi Sierra!" I smiled. Living on the edge, not knowing what would happen next, taking a leap of faith. How appropriate.

I pondered, "What would her middle name be?" My husband's father, Burtell, had passed away from colon cancer when Andy was four years old. This was devastating for him. He shared with me a few memories of his dad. One he held so dear was the concept of telling time with him. He recalled his father being sick and in bed a lot, as he had a serious illness. There was a void in Andy's life. He hadn't experienced those special times with him growing up as father and son. Thankfully, his loving uncle stepped in as a positive role model for him. He remained a prominent force in his life.

I sensed Burtell's spirit around, quite often. It was as though he walked a few steps behind Andy keeping a watchful eye on him. Good things happened for Andy at work and throughout those many arduous marathons and climbs. He had his health and he persevered. Andy's mother and uncle shared how kind his dad was. A "B" name was essential. I looked up names beginning with this letter. I found the name Brooke; meaning—small stream. The jagged edge of a mountain leading into a small stream. Sierra Brooke-Simply, beautiful.

Living on the Edge

Living on the edge was something my husband adhered to, at least in relation to extra-curricular activities. Climbing Mt. Kilimanjaro in Tanzania was far from an easy feat. It held a profound significance for Andy. This was just prior to his fortieth birthday, the same age his dad had passed. Andy chose to partake in this, as it was an experience that offered him a deeper awareness, in his connection with his father. As he made his way to the top of the mountain, he found a more gratifying state of grace.

Andy climbed many more mountains. Also, he ran the course of eighteen marathons. His motivation was attributed to his passion to support others in raising funds for children who suffered from leukemia. Andy was committed to helping people achieve their dreams, for them to thrive in whatever their passions were, and for their greatest potentials to manifest. He was a peacemaker who experienced joy, simply being in the company of others. He delighted in conversation.

Even though Andy was a type A personality in many ways, he was accepting of others. Although I was driven, I was inclined to appreciate a slower pace. I was meticulous and cautious about certain things, especially when it was more intimate at heart. I reminded myself, there was only so much one could prepare. Sometimes, I had to take a leap of faith.

Turning Further In

I walked almost every day throughout three seasons. Since Sierra was an April baby, there were many months before the warmer weather arrived. I bundled myself up in my light blue down parka winter coat, delighted in keeping my baby warm. It was an exhilarating experience, walking in the crisp air, taking in the sights and sounds of nature, knowing Sierra was within me.

I hadn't paid much attention to how much I was increasing in weight, even though I was slowly and steadily. I wasn't on any specific regimen or restrictive caloric diet. I was conscious of my overall health. I enjoyed eating organic fruits and vegetables, quinoa, as well as other gluten free grains. Sometimes, I craved some crispy delectable french fries with a juicy medium-well hamburger. Perhaps, it was iron I was lacking. I hadn't deprived myself of ice cream and dark chocolate, which I really could not part from. Mostly, I was interested in obtaining nutrients from organic food sources, as that was the best way to absorb vitamins. I was careful to avoid fruits and vegetables sprayed with chemicals and avoided genetically modified foods. I ate hormone free chicken and a variety of fish for omega's and healthy fats.

I took a few supplements-a multi-vitamin, vitamin B and C, daily, mineral water, a probiotic, and vitamin D. Since the folic acid tablets were making me feel a little nauseous, I stopped taking these. I used chemical free soaps and shampoos without parabens and fillers. I cleaned our home with natural ingredients containing lemon, eucalyptus, and apple cider vinegar. Also, I refrained from highlighting my hair throughout my entire pregnancy. I visited an organic salon for a haircut, around every four months.

Still, it concerned me that my immune system could have a negative impact upon my child's overall health. I contracted mononucleosis at ten years old. I hadn't known how on earth I would contract that. It could have been from a water fountain, I suppose. From the time I was fourteen years old, I developed pulsating headaches and sinus problems from chemical sensitivities. I found out from an allergist that I was allergic to dust, mold, cats and dogs. Other diagnoses I was given were, Chronic Fatigue Syndrome, Epstein Barr Virus, or a questionable interpretation that a top neurologist shared with me, as "causes, mostly unknown or stress related". After college, I diagnosed myself with having candidiasis. Its symptomologies included, brain fog and digestive issues. It provoked me to become more aware of how our food consumption and environment impacted our health.

My healing journey took a turn for the better when I moved to Southern California. I was twenty-two years old. It was the haven for progressive living and overall health. I discovered gluten free products, as gluten, a protein found in wheat, was causing me brain fog, headaches, and bloating. I visited a local health food store daily. I felt I could live a more satisfying way of life, as they sold grains that I could actually, eat. Rice, quinoa, and millet became a staple of mine. My goal was to get well, so I eliminated many processed foods and refined sugars. In addition, I alternated between receiving acupuncture treatments and chiropractic care. On most mornings, I jogged on the beach.

After a couple of years, I wanted to return to school for a masters, in art therapy. It was a degree that wasn't offered in any of the colleges, nearby. I decided to move back home, and enroll in a college, nearby family. I continued being committed to my diet, exercise, and a life path which included cleanses, yoga, meditation, and prayer. It was an ongoing process.

To Have and to Hold

As a child, I lived in a high ranch house in a tiny hamlet of a suburban town. One might infer that I was kind of sheltered in a way. Growing up in the seventies, life was in a sense, simpler, then. There were less pressures to excel at sports and academia. Children ran around in their backyards, rode bikes and played outside. There was a more cohesive community and personalization without the use of technology clouding socialization. Less opportunities were available for purposes of distraction. Sitting down with family at dinner without turning to a cell phone, or a computer held greater value.

I enjoyed family time. Even though our lives weren't perfect, my parents taught me respect for others, and were giving and thoughtful. My dad worked late on some evenings, so my mom, sister and I would be in each other's company. Going to dinner and shopping on Friday nights at the mall was a typical outing of ours. It was enjoyable for me, mainly because we were together.

The experiences we had with my dad, whether it be barbecuing on the weekends, family outings with friends, or going to the shore during our summers off, I treasured. Celebrating birthdays and holidays with extended family meant so much to me.

However, within the scope of influence my parents had upon me, some things I couldn't ignore;

My mom, Jane, suffered from anxiety. Merging on a parkway was a huge ordeal. Mom turned off the radio, so that she could intently, focus on her driving. Her voice quickened, as she nervously, asked us to be quiet.

At nine years of age, when I walked home from school, each step I took led me closer towards the doorway where I would meet up with something larger than I could handle. My heart beat out of my chest. I hurried to get there. The sooner I would arrive, the sooner it would be over. As I reached to turn the knob of our front door, I took in a huge breath of air. The anxiousness in my mother's voice pulsated through me. "Hi Marn—You're home!" It sounded like partial excitement, and partial relief that I was home safely. The tone of voice and erratic nature emanating from her was intense, at times. It wasn't every day. Yet, it happened. I swallowed it and gulped it down.

At about five years old, my parents signed me up for ice skating. When I fell on the ice during one of the early sessions, my mom hurriedly swept me off the rink. I never returned for more lessons.

I took piano lessons with my older sister, Jill. Even though I loved the way the piano sounded, I had little motivation to practice. Once, I made a little goodie bag for my teacher, so he would not be upset with me. His voice, the gold necklace he wore, with a buttoned-down shirt, where I could see some of his hairy chest, reminded me of Neil Diamond. I greatly enjoyed listening to him play, however he emitted a strong body odor, so it was difficult to sit adjacent to him. Soon after, my parents signed my sister and me up with a woman who taught piano in her home. She was talented and had a beautiful voice; however, her house permeated from the smell of cats. She must have had, at least five. One day when we were over for a lesson, she got up frequently, to enter into the kitchen. She returned with a small shot glass, followed by taking a swig of it. We called our parents to pick us up, which of course, they did. About a week later, we received an apology letter in the mail confessing that she was at a party the night, prior. We decided not to resume sessions with her. We hadn't pursued piano lessons, after that.

In hindsight, I saw that my mother was afraid for me to fall. As a baby, prior to taking that first step, wiggling and wobbling was all part of the learning process—It was necessary to have an ample amount of "woopsie doos", while mastering the art of it. Like the old familiar tale of Humpty Dumpty—"All the king's horses and all the king's men couldn't put humpty dumpty back together again." The falling in itself, was indeed beautiful.

The endearing qualities my mother held, I admired;
- Mom was funny. Sometimes, she dressed up in outfits and entertained us and her best friend who lived across the street. She wanted attention. I understood that, and I got a kick out this, and her enjoyment of it.
- Mom was smart. An excellent writer. She wrote poetry and whimsical songs. She took pride in singing them, as well. Many had rhyming verses. I loved hearing them.

— Mom showed me she had courage. When I was ten years of age, my mom returned to school. She enrolled in a program to obtain her nursing degree. I was proud of her for having the confidence to do so, especially being in her mid-thirties, and after having children. Mom worked at a hospital in orthopedics for years. Then, later used her skills obtaining a job as a case manager for a couple of different active community senior centers. She was responsible and maintained steady jobs in her field.

Throughout the years many issues weren't discussed, or addressed, and were swept under the rug, or simply avoided. When I was fourteen years old, I recommended that we all attend family therapy sessions. Mom didn't think it was necessary and encouraged me to go on my own. She explained that she didn't need therapy and was too old for it. I didn't understand. In my eyes, she was young, only twenty-six years older than me. Mom's reluctance to attending therapy sessions, spilled over into other areas. I concluded that our bond as mother and daughter wasn't worth it, and it wasn't strong enough to compel her to work on her own issues.

My mother's fears I held within me, like a glass jar. I felt responsible for protecting her from the outside world, and in some ways, myself. I retreated to a place where I had to determine my own healthful boundaries, and sense of self in terms of trust and commitment. The pressure to have things look status quo on the outside, was necessary in painting a pretty picture.

My dad, Robin, was a rather optimistic person, always smiling, very congenial. He was somewhat reserved with a quiet temperament, friendly and warm. When my mom experienced an anxiety attack, he situated himself in the same spot on the couch, appearing almost frozen. The pain of watching my mother in a panicked state, while my father sat silently, as if he were waiting for it to disappear, made me run inside.

Still, my dad would do just about anything for me, for anyone for that matter. He would buy food for a homeless man. He would give to various charities. He was always lending a hand. Dad was a lithographer, quite artistic with a keen eye for detail. He was meticulous. Walking into my parent's garage was like being in a ready to be sold apartment that was just cleaned. The tools and trinkets on the shelving units upon the walls were in exact equidistance from each other. Everything had its place.

My sister, Jill, was shy of being a couple of years older than me. Sisters shared a sacred bond with one another. I believed they could tell the other just about anything. My sister was reluctant in expressing more with me about her experiences. I thought it would be innate for her to be comfortable with me, to trust me, as her loving sister. We valued similar topics; the environment, animals, health, and a more peaceable world. I longed for a deeper exchange in terms of communication with her. She was my sister. I loved her.

If emotions were not shared, nothing could rock the boat. Avoiding discussions of bigger issues, while pushing down things of critical importance, until they toppled over was not a healthful way of approaching real life situations. It was a lesson in disguise, although it would show up and manifest in different ways. I was expressive, so being a part of a family that was inexpressive was very difficult for me. I had a quiet temperament, with an introspective outlook. I wanted to please my parents, as children typically do, for them to be more accepting of me. Life was not perfect. Addressing feelings was integral to self-growth.

Birth Day

Undulant waves surged forward, then back again. As they escalated more intensely, I tried to embrace the sharp pains pulsating through me. I breathed in and out consciously, with rapidity.

I knew it was time—My husband calculated the contractions. He remembered the method of this from our birthing class. As he looked down at his watch, he pressed the seconds button to determine the amount of time in between each interval. This helped us in figuring out how long we needed to wait before we arrived at the hospital. Our doula, Christine, recommended remaining in the comforts of our home for as long as we could. She would be of assistance to us, throughout the course of my labor. The hospital we chose had a good reputation and was close to where we resided.

In the wee hours of the morn on April 8th, the moment arrived. I rolled out of bed, slowly making my way down what seemed like a long staircase. Andy held out his hand to assist me, as I steadily made my way into his car. It was dusky outside. When we arrived, just as we pulled up to the waiting area in the emergency room, an attendant came over. The minutes seemed like they tripled. Andy graciously took my hand, as I wobbled over into a wheelchair. I struggled to sit down before another contraction came.

It was all very surreal. My baby was on her way. The nurse, also a midwife, entered our room. She was thorough in creating our birth plan early on in my pregnancy. It felt reassuring that it was about to be executed. It entailed a natural childbirth, one without the use of any drugs. I would be coherent and fully awake remembering years later, that very first moment looking into my babies' eyes, while holding her close.

As I laid propped up on the small rectangular hospital bed, I acclimated myself as best I could. It didn't matter that the room was stark white and clean. The large windows allowed in a good amount of light. A nurse came in and introduced herself. She was soft-spoken and friendly. Her kind demeanor made me feel more at ease. Upon reading my chart, she noticed my birthday was on July 11th. It was the same day as hers. Shortly after, our doula Christine arrived, two women with the same name. Surely, I was being looked after. Divine intervention.

Dr. Dawson arrived in our room. I was comforted by the fact that he was wearing worn out blue jeans and a white polo shirt. Nonchalantly, he shared that he was on his way to a golf match, however decided to detour and come here, instead. He figured this was more important. Dr. Dawson's humor was contagious. I couldn't help but laugh. The rest of the staff in the room chuckled, amused by his entertaining way.

I watched the minutes move, ever so slowly, on the large clock on the wall adjacent to my bed. Bathed in sweat and all sticky, this had been consuming me. I was feeling sapped of energy. My contractions increased in frequency from three to eight centimeters, in about an hour and a half. Ten would come around soon, I surmised. I had been in such pain. Although the hours were passing, it seemed like days. When it came time to having to use the bathroom, Andy steadily took my hand, assisting me out of bed, along with my doula. Thankfully, it was only a few feet away. Just as I had finished, without any hesitancy, I drop kicked the toilet. Both of them laughed hysterically. I was merely, being polite.

Hurriedly, I got into bed and back to work! This was beyond, tough. I closed my eyes and imagined being under the covers, listening to soothing music and eating vanilla bean ice cream, my favorite flavor with dark chocolate chips. My baby was enjoying herself, until now, that is. I rustled her world. Why should she have to come out from being in this comfy state of bliss? It was TIME. I did what I HAD to do. I rocked myself back and forth attempting to relieve the excruciating agony and to propel me to speed up the process.

I advocated for a bathtub to be of use for those giving birth at the hospital. Unfortunately, it wasn't implemented, yet. However, I had the luxury of utilizing the shower, which at one point I gravitated to. During my short time in there, which lasted only for about minute or two, I had this very ungrounded sensation. Quickly, I got out and returned to what was more supportive for me. The hard quality of the mattress on the small rectangular bed provided a more secure foundation. I focused even more, intensely, as I moved within a rhythm. I immersed myself, as I got into a zone. I repositioned my body. I knelt down, moving up like a cat, and back down into the cow position. Being in a trance like state, voices were sounding more muffled. Still, I could hear the staff sharing how calm I was. I focused on being calm! I breathed inwards and outwards, trying to relax. I looked up hourly, pacing myself. An exasperating experience, it seemed like forever.

At one point, after another grueling push, I thought about the prospect of having a cesarean. Being in excruciating pain, I gathered whatever energy I had and in a wispy like voice cried out, "I feel like I'm going to die." I couldn't take the pain any longer, and so I did the next best thing. I closed my eyes, tightly-with great intent. I prayed more than I ever had! As if I were in this lucid dreaming kind of state, still conscious, a beautiful image swept through me. It was of my baby's soulful eyes, as we melted into a warm embrace. All of a sudden, I heard the team cheering, "There's her crown. There's her head!"

Breathing and pushing—"Just a little more", I heard. At that critical point, the struggle had ceased. The endorphins must have kicked in. I heard the most glorious cry! I watched my baby being bundled up in a soft white blanket. Tears drizzled down my face into the sides of my mouth. I looked into my daughter's beautiful sparkling eyes, as she nestled her sweet plush pink body into mine. Like waves resurfacing, her heart beat, in sync with mine.

All too soon, Sierra was disengaged from my cocooned like embrace. I watched the nurse place her on the cold hard scale. I was inclined as a new mother to scoop her up, nurture, and protect her. Shortly after, the nurse walked over and placed my baby back into my welcoming arms. My husband wheeled us back to our private room. Andy was leaving for a short while. He was preparing our babies room at home. Also, the heat wasn't working, and he wanted to be certain it was fixed upon our arrival.

Despite being fatigued, it was difficult for me to sleep. I was kind of antsy, and preferred being in the comforts of my home. Even though I was in a private room, I was distracted by the sounds of machines beeping, and the bright light emanating through the doorway. Nurses poked their heads in from time to time, perhaps to check in on me, which I appreciated. When I finally drifted, it was for a short period. I was a light sleeper. As the nurses changed shifts, they wrote their names on the wipe board, adjacent to my bed.

A nurse came in to bring Sierra outside to check her vitals, blood pressure, etc. I thought about who would be holding her, keeping her safe. The hands on the clock wall moved, ever so slowly. It was a much longer wait then I expected. The nurse shared they were returning her, at least an hour sooner. I was concerned. Also, it was feeding time. Perhaps, they were delayed because there was a plethora of babies born that day. When they weighed her earlier, I noticed every scale had been utilized. They had referred to Sierra as being a "leap frog", as she was only five pounds. It was a term they coined for newborn weighing somewhere between what a preemie was and a full-sized baby.

Maybe, she was in an incubator or on a table wrapped up, seeking the protection of her mama bear holding her, keeping her warm. The seconds that turned into minutes evolved into an hour. After about eight hours, they returned with Sierra. They ran some routine tests. Our "bundle of joy" was returned to me. Our doula, Christine, called her this term of endearment when Sierra first arrived. It resonated with me.

Being able to nurse Sierra came easily, as she instantly, latched on. When it came time for me to use the laboratory, the nurse offered her help. Upon lifting her, a couple of times, she sensed that Sierra was heavier than what was on her hospital bracelet. She left to reweigh her. Upon returning, she nodded with a chuckle of certainty, "Five pounds, six ounces." I was surprised they made a mistake like that, especially since they coined her a leap frog. Perhaps, they wouldn't have run certain tests. Just then, I recalled that I took a picture of Sierra when she was just born and weighed her on the scale. It read four pounds, sixteen ounces. We decided to declare her original weight at five pounds, seven ounces. I figured she could have lost an ounce due to water weight. Most importantly, she was healthy.

After being at the hospital for a couple of days, I was discharged. So excited to be taking our baby home, I bundled her up in her rose-colored outfit. A petite knitted white hat covered the newness of her softer than a feather, plush scalp. I placed it over her delicate pinkish blush ears. Her ensemble was just a little large for her small frame, even with the preemie sized onesies my mom and dad brought back for us. How sweet she was, so perfect. A euphoric sensation traveled through me, as I snuggled her up in my arms. I walked out that door with a love I had never felt before. I was home.

Healthy Child

In the early months of Sierra's life, that wonderfully succulent aroma of her pure essence filled me with such delight. A gift from mother nature's bounties. It opened my eyes to something greater than I had ever imagined. As I placed her delicate body upon mine, it was heavenly.

I played all kinds of music from lullabies, to folk, to classical, to pop. I sang to her in as melodic voice as I could. It was soft, higher pitched, and somewhat child-like. My grandmother Miriam's youthful tone was similar. She was my greatest role model—youthful, joyous, and quite theatrical. She loved learning about people and their interests, simply interacting with them. She walked every day to the little avenue surrounding her apartment and partook in her daily exercises. I aspired to be like her. Sierra was blessed to have a great grandmother and one such as she, the wisest woman I knew.

As I peered into those soulful eyes, here in this tranquil place, life slowed down. This relaxed state could have been in part caused by the oxytocin and prolactin glands, the hormones produced from breastfeeding. Thankfully, during this time those endorphins kicked in. Even though waking up in the wee hours of the morning was tough, as soon as I peeked into Sierra's room and saw that angelic face, all worries melted away. There was no greater love than being a mother.

My focus was on providing Sierra with a solid foundation to build upon. Walks around the neighborhood were a daily encounter. We'd stroll around the cul-de-sac, up a small hill and around the bend in her Bugaboo stroller. This was a favorite activity of ours. Since Sierra was born in April, the spring like weather was favorable. There was less bundling up. It was easier to get in and out of the house. Also, we lived in a fairly slow-moving area which was comforting, a suburban town with a bit of a rural feel. Sidewalks and lots of trees surrounded us. People were friendly. We made friends with a few of our neighbors. One very loving and kind family was a couple of houses up from us. They had two daughters. They would often be outside playing in the yard. They were around six and eight years old, at the time Sierra was born. Our neighbor across the street was very nurturing and she truly loved babies. She offered her help, whenever we needed it.

Maggie, our pup, was a great companion. She enjoyed playing with some of the dogs on the street. Maggie was trained rather well by a reputable company shortly after Sierra was born. It was kind of like a light boot camp for dogs. For two weeks a dedicated, kind, and smart young lady arrived at our home, reinforcing goals she practiced with Maggie. Maggie was rather easy, so incredibly smart. She gave Sierra just enough space, as if she knew that she was part of her pack, of her family. The training got easier as the days passed. Maggie was a sensitive, affectionate little dog. I often referred to her as "my furry baby" and Sierra's "furry sister". I savored these special moments.

Holistic Doctor

We chose a holistic doctor. Two mothers who had a vested interest in health recommended her. One of the employees who worked at our local health food store informed us that she had given workshops there. She had been practicing as a doctor for many years. After doing some research, we made an appointment with her. The doctor reviewed a few vaccines she considered to be of greater importance. She had not commented about what age she would recommend giving these. She eluded to that fact that she was open to hearing our thoughts and acknowledging our choices, even if we were opposed to taking vaccines or in delaying the allotted schedule.

When Sierra was shy of four months of age, we scheduled a routine doctor's visit. I arrived with our daughter at the pediatrician's office. I was enamored by Sierra's innocence. I observed her, tucked into the blanket in her little seat. So serene.

I was optimistic about Sierra's health as well as, being confident in the doctor. The receptionist looked over, and in a gentle and soft voice informed us that the doctor would be out shortly. She had a consoling way, as she remembered the days of being a new mom and offered her help. If I needed some time for me, she offered to provide me with her babysitter's number. Even though I was fatigued, I knew it was part of being a new mom. I was thankful to her, however maybe sometime in the future.

After my name was called, we were led into a small room. As soon as I entered, I took out some toiletries. It was changing time. The doctor was respectful and left the room, allowing us some privacy. As soon as she returned, she took a small tube out of a bag. It was a vaccine. I was a little jittery and unprepared for this. She tried to alleviate any doubts, with confidence that it wouldn't harm her. I gathered that it was one vaccine, so I assumed it would be okay. A short while after, she removed another vial from a bag. Curiously, I asked her what it was. She shared it was the Rotavirus. When I probed for more information, as I wasn't so comfortable with giving her this, she reassured me that I had nothing to worry about. "It's like giving a little sugar water".

What? It's not really a vaccine? Sugar water? Before I could open my mouth to say "no", in the bleep of an instant she gave this to her, orally. Then, she replied in an abrupt, strong manner, bearing a Russian accent—"Take thuja!" I was Russian, so in no way was I undermining her. However, she invalidated my questions and concerns. "Take thuja?" It was like a tracer being given after a swig of rum. How odd to have suggested a homeopathic remedy right after giving her this, as if there could be complications or side effects. She commented that she had recently began attending classes for her homeopathic certification. How could she know what remedy to give her? Surely, there were homeopathic remedies available to the general public for purchase in holistic markets, but this was serious. Most homeopaths that were classically trained would take a history for an hour or two before determining a more accurately based, constitutional remedy.

The thought occurred to me, whether she was a western or an eastern doctor. Was she more mainstream or holistic? It was as if she had served us fruit roll up pops on one hand, and apples on the other. It was like she was haphazardly experimenting with my daughter's life, while she obtained her homeopathic certification. When I returned home, I decided to read up on thuja. I was worried about giving her two vaccines at once, even though in her very own words, one was like a little "sugar water". I read that one of thuja's benefits was to counteract any negative effects from vaccines. I picked it up from the health food store when my daughter was crying for a short while. I gave Sierra a low dose containing a couple of pellets of the remedy. I diluted it in some water. Honestly, I wasn't sure what effect it had.

The doctor acted forthright and inflexible. Giving two vaccines, concurrently, wasn't sitting well with me. One was enough for a baby's tiny body to process. Perhaps, this was a premonition I held deep within shouting at me to be more careful. I felt disrespected in her reluctance to hear my concerns and value what I was saying, especially as a new mother doing her best to be cautious.

Doc

From the time Sierra was six weeks old, we took her in to see one of our dearest friends. He was one of my go to people that had remained a constant in my life. He was our chiropractor, whom we referred to as "Doc". I had been using his services for about ten years. Always smiling; he was a peaceable, jovial, and attentive man. I admired him. He married twice. Both had passed away from cancer. His second wife, he truly adored—She was diagnosed with ovarian cancer during her pregnancy. The duration of her illness was not long. At the same time, he was tending to her needs, he was providing for his young daughter diagnosed with Rett syndrome. His office was downstairs in his home, as it was favorable for him to be in closer proximity to his daughter. He gave optimal care to his patient's and always emerged with an optimistic attitude.

When Doc evaluated Sierra, he commented, mostly that she was so healthy. We were contented in his analysis and felt reassured. We also discussed my diet, as well as Sierra's, and any supplements like vitamin D, mineral water, and adding silver water for any viral or bacterial issues, among others. Doc used kinesiology to determine courses of action, as well as, our next appointment. We would visit accordingly, from anywhere from four to eight weeks, typically.

When Sierra was about six months old, Doc noticed some flacidity in Sierra's hands. He didn't think it was anything major to be concerned about as she was still an infant. He shared with us that from a developmental perspective that there was a bell curve, and it wasn't always so well defined, as on an exact schedule. It made me realize even more, that not everything was going to be perfect according to a book's guidelines. Nature would take its course. Still, there were times I grew concerned.

Weeks passed before we saw Doc, again for treatment. It had been a couple of months. He had noticed that Sierra was more compromised and delayed in her motor development, especially in her wrists and upper portion of her hands. She had been hypotonic, which meant she had reduced pressure or tone. He encouraged us to continue what we were doing for Sierra to use her whole body, as we did different occupational types of movement: pulling and pushing objects, reaching and grasping for objects, playing catch; anything to support her growth in this area.

Mommy and Me

Sierra Brooke, a sweet-blessed child, was more than I could have ever imagined. Such an elated feeling, as I lifted her precious body upwards and downwards, peering into those darling eyes. That endearing smile was so innocent, and hearing her babble was such a delight to hear. We listened to all kinds of music. Sierra bopped around in her seat and got into the groove, as she moved back and forth to the sounds of the beat.

At around five months of age, Sierra and I joined a mommy and me music class.

Our first music class was led by an instructor from a program called Music Together®. It was at a local church in an affluent town next to where we resided.

I was excited for us to be a part of this community socializing with other parents and learning about them. After being home alone for hours at a time, away from the familiar routine of sleeping, changing her, and nursing for many hours a day, this was a real treat. Even though it took a substantial amount of time to get us ready, it was part of a mom's world. After feeding her, packing up diapers, and belongings, it was well worth the trip.

We sat in a circle with our children. As I situated our sweet little angel in front of me, I propped her up on my lap on a large semi-soft rug. She would clasp the egg shakers with her tiny hands, as she coordinated movements in a rhythmic type way. After a few sessions, the teacher commented how attentive and alert Sierra was.

One mother and I became instant friends. Melanie introduced me to her daughter Grace. Grace exhibited a sweet, delicate quality about her. Soon after, Melanie confided that Grace was a preemie at birth. She was a little concerned about this, however she was reassured that she was developing rather, well. She was bright eyed and alert with an engaging smile and had an adoring personality.

Melanie had a maturity about her. When she told me that she was in her late forties, I admired her for having the stamina and willingness to commit to motherhood. During class, we chatted. We treasured these precious moments we shared with each other. It was consoling, as new mothers validating the essential encounters we were going through.

I was thrilled Sierra had made a little friend. How wonderful it would be years later to reflect upon a friendship, from early on. Our children would have a unique bond. Melanie and I saw each other from time to time. We enjoyed walks at a local park next to a library and a playground area.

Venturing out more into public places required more effort and dedication than I had thought. I was breastfeeding. I hadn't used a pump until Sierra was about six months old. The more I nourished her, the more I produced. Sierra was growing by leaps and bounds. If I wasn't diligent with feeding times, my ducts could swell up from overproducing.

When I shared my concerns with Melanie, it wasn't apparent that she had a clear understanding of what I had been experiencing, and she didn't express much in regard to, empathizing with this. Melanie was busy, and added on more work hours, with limited time to meet up. Our calls became less frequent. I bumped into her from time to time and we would discuss meeting up. Though we were amicable and open to it, neither of us followed through. It was sad to part with this friendship, though I knew people came into our lives for different reasons, and to learn from each other.

I continued participating in a variety of classes, enjoying these special moments with Sierra. During our mommy and me yoga class, Sierra would move about with a curiosity about her. Other children seemed a little less distracted. This was about the time she was around six to eight months old.

The first day we attended a different music class the instructor passed out post it notes. She asked us to write our names on it. Just next to me, there was a woman whose name read, "Cecilia's mom." Something about this made me wonder about how much she valued her own identity. Even though Sierra was my dear child, whom I loved unconditionally, having a sense of individuality was important to me.

At about thirteen months of age during a music class, I noticed some of the other children articulating sounds and words, pointing, and waving. Sierra glided about the room as she picked up a few instruments. She walked around and back, again. A woman was viewing her cell phone. Sierra walked over to her. She seemed fixated on obtaining it, as she reached out her hand and attempted to take hold of it. I went over to the woman to apologize to her. She thought nothing of it, rather found it to be sweet and innocent.

Passages of Time

I reflected on Sierra's milestones. Often, she reached for things, as she moved about the room. Sierra's first words were "Good Girl". She sounded it out—"Goo-wa-d G-i-w-l." It warmed my heart. She viewed books for hours. She marveled at all the colors in them, as she babbled and made noises. The books with pictures of people and feelings, she pulled out, pointing at the pictures. She especially loved safari animals. She said, "Lio" for Lion and "Dada-dada". Oh, how she loved her daddy. Andy often went outside with her, as he took out her little red wagon and pulled her around the sidewalk. They swung around our quaint neighborhood alongside our loyal little pup, Maggie. Sierra appreciated nature and the outdoors. She was a typical toddler running, jumping and playing in the grass, inquisitive and bold. She was entertained by cause and effect toys, different shaped and sounding blocks, pushing and pulling her own wooden wagon, puzzles, and Baby Einstein videos. She propelled herself around the room, sometimes scooting about it by using the small table and couches, or anything else she could grasp onto. She was quite coordinated.

As the months passed, I noticed that Sierra's words were somewhat stilted and jumbled with partial sounds or prefixes or where only suffixes of words were formed. Her articulation and pronunciation were more compromised than I had noticed prior. I watched her subtle movements and sounds as she sat or hustled over to the shelfing unit at the far wall nearest the corner adjacent to the large windowsill. She was meticulous about turning the pages of her books. Often, she left them open-expressing her thoughts. Sometimes, it appeared as if she was perseverating on turning the pages. Her interest in the Baby Einstein videos increased. Even though they were musically inviting, I was mindful they could be over stimulating.

Typically, my parents visited us, once every two to three weeks. They lived about two and a half hours south of us. Grandma was overjoyed to see her precious grandchild. I was grateful for her coming. She was warm and friendly to her, and very enthusiastic in speaking with her. There was nothing like having a grandma around.

One day Grandma and Grandpa visited when Sierra was about fifteen months old. My mom called out to Sierra, yet she hadn't responded. She exclaimed, "She doesn't know me." "She doesn't know my name!" Although this shook me up a little, I shrugged at the idea of it being anything significant. Besides, Sierra was young and perhaps, introspective which wasn't so odd, especially if she was anything like me.

I began to take note of my family history. No one had any diagnoses for intellectual issues. The handful of genetic tests we had participated in prior to Sierra's birth were normal. A couple of the blood tests were given to us for determining what could be prevalent for any problems, on the basis of our nationalities. Andy's and mine was that of Jewish descent. Sierra was so young. Although I had little experience with children under two years of age, I was aware that each of us learn at our own pace. I thought about the developmental milestones on the sheet given to us at the pediatrician's office. Prior to Sierra's last couple of check-ups, I was a little quick in filling out the forms. I gathered she knew how to perform certain tasks, like catching a ball and throwing it, pointing at things to show me, etc. However, I wasn't going to turn a blind's eye. I began to consider the idea that I was missing something.

Health Review

I thought about my health and all that I experienced prior to conceiving. I reviewed what I had eaten prior to birth. I had detoxed myself with about twelve cleanses over the course of two years. Hulda Clarke was a medical doctor that produced this rather intricate protocol to cleanse the liver. It consisted of drinking grapefruit juice and epsom salt over a twenty-four hour period. A period of rest was essential, the day following. I cleaned out my system as best I could, healing my gut and any allergies.

Holistic was so much a part of my lifestyle. Just prior to and after getting pregnant, I attended the Le Leche League and joined a group called the Holistic Moms Network of New Jersey. I ate mostly organic, however not a purely, vegetarian diet. I consumed fish daily consuming those beneficial omega oils and ate poultry for protein.

I continued limiting my sugars and refrained from eating gluten. I purchased organic produce. I pureed Sierra's baby food. She loved avocadoes, sweet potatoes, split peas, and pears. A balanced diet was best. Naturally, she began eating more solid foods. Rice, quinoa, and fish were part of that, veggies and fruits. Also, I ate fairly healthy during this time, mostly organic. I drank coffee however; it was only one or two cups a day. I had been more of a tea drinker, up until the time Sierra was born. Yet, the black and green tea were not doing the trick, in terms of keeping me awake. I continued nursing Sierra up until she approached the thirteen-month mark. I gave her soy and rice milk. I hadn't wanted to give her dairy or milk from a cow that could be hard to assimilate. I looked at Sierra in awe of her tenacity and inward beauty. I would do all I could to be diligent in supplying her with a healthful approach in body, mind, and spirit.

Waking Up to Something More

It was at the mark of Sierra's fifteen-month check-up we had seen Dr. Chen, our pediatrician at Mile High Pediatrics. We had switched to this practice when Sierra was six months old. These were doctors that encouraged us to continue with the vaccines and reassured us that there weren't any conclusive studies about them causing damage to our systems. The doctors refuted anything that was reported as vaccines causing neurological impairments. They shared that it was debunked. I was not going to be brainwashed into a societal world, where drugs were typically the answer before a more natural way of proceeding with diet, supplements, and exercise.

My husband, Andy, responded in a rather fearful way concerning vaccines, "I work in the city", "You never know what viruses I can contract." I debated about giving Sierra more vaccines. I spaced them out, mostly one at a time. There were a couple of times, I had given her two. The first was that sugar water vaccine. The second time I felt pressured, as I was told by the doctors that

I way behind on a few of the shots. At this point, Sierra had three shots of the rotavirus, three shots of the Hib, three shots of DTaP, and three shots of Prevnar. That was a total of twelve shots in a span of fifteen months. Still, the number of shots Sierra had been given was not nearly what the doctors suggested. The proposed schedule for Sierra's vaccinations was at least double the number we had given her.

Dr. Chen shared in a very concerned manner, "I notice Sierra isn't making all her milestones." "She isn't waving to me, pointing to me, or responding to my name." I sank deeper into a place that was grimmer than I had ever known. As if I was, being pulled towards the bottom of the ocean soon to be wedged underneath a rock, alongside coral reefs without any sort of relief.

The doctor reached out her hand, one that seemed larger than life, as if it were from some outer galactic green goblin. She offered me something scribbled on a small strip of paper. Words I tried to deflect. I turned my head. My whole body was coiling up, as I tried to maintain my composure. I could taste the saltiness of a tear drop streaming down my face. Her voice sounding more muffled, as if I were caught in another space. Riveting pains penetrated through me. I glanced at the piece of paper. It contained the number for early intervention, and a developmental pediatrician's name with the hospital she resided at.

As I walked out of that office, I knew our lives had changed, forever. It was as though a dagger had stuck me in my heart. I asked for a sign—any sign to let me know that Sierra would be okay. Shaken up, I managed to open up the car door. Gently, I placed her in the car seat. When I buckled her in and heard that click, it was as though reality set in. I proceeded to position myself, as comfortably as I could. Though nothing could provide any sort of solace in this dark, unfamiliar place.

I put my car in reverse, my foot on the brake. Just as I peered outside my window, something compelled me to turn around. It was in that instant, that Sierra spoke the most beautiful word I had ever heard—"milk!" I breathed in a sigh of relief. A sign, a glimmer of hope was on the horizon. Still, I braced myself. I pulled out of that parking lot in preparation for the long road ahead.

The Shot of What If

I ruminated time and time again. "WHAT IF?" What if I didn't give my daughter those vaccines? What if I stood up to these, so called educated pediatricians and said, "NO?" Instead, it was like hit or miss on the dartboard. "Here you go… Here's a shot for you! A shot in the gut. A shot in the dark. A shot in your child's development. A shot in her LIFE!"

I put my trust in the hands of well-versed doctors. I wanted to believe that my baby would be okay. However, perhaps doctors were being driven by the mercy of what one could obtain, lucratively, and out of fear. Living in a false paradigm with directives from insurance companies that per vaccine, doctors would receive a payment of y, if you followed this x. Why hadn't the doctors shown me the bag with the ingredients listed that were in the vaccines? The FDA and Big Pharma companies knew what was in them, along with many doctors and politicians. To be injecting this concoction that contained preservatives, aborted fetal tissue, aluminum, MF59, mercury, thimerosal, antibiotics, egg proteins, yeast proteins, human cell strains, animal cell strains and GMO's could be detrimental. Our country was depleted of nutrients and most of us were toxic in some way to the point where our systems were not able to handle these harmful substances. Generation upon generation, we were void of some healthful strains of bacteria, and our guts and our immune systems were compromised. We lived in a world where there was so much waste generated from genetically modified foods, and our water supply. Also, global warming, air pollution, urban sprawl, ozone layer pollution, waste disposal, acid rain, climate change, would affect humans, animals and every nation.

Knowing the state of our health, as a society we needed to be more cautious as to what we were putting into our bodies. This is from the moment we are born. We have to ask ourselves, why weren't there blood tests administered to determine whether there are methylation issues, allergenic responses to ingredients, or a compromised immune system? A baby's nervous system is not developed until six to eight months of age, which may not assimilate chemicals and unnatural ingredients within their tiny bodies. I wondered, "Why are there barely any holistic pediatricians in our county?" I knew of one, besides the pediatrician we had seen. We opted not to go there, as it was relatively far from home.

Calling All Angels

I picked up the phone, s-l-o-w-l-y. Hands tense, uneasy. It was as if I was dialing 911. This emergent feeling, I had. It had been about two weeks, since I picked up that little piece of paper from the pediatrician. I dared to call early intervention and reach out to the experts. "Couldn't I do this on my own?" Couldn't I get my baby's life back—All I thought about was healing her from the pain compromising her mind and body. I wanted an answer and a quick one, at that.

Even though I would receive assistance, there was a resistance inside of me that shielded me from believing any of this was happening. I was compelled to cancel before the women from early intervention arrived. I wanted to say with certainty, "Thank you. I'm good. She's fine. All is well."

Scared, confused, and somewhat depressed, the troop came a knockin' at our door. I was greeted by a case manager, a speech therapist, and a special education teacher. The company was approved by the state education department. Children between ages birth through three who had scored above a twenty-fifth percentile in an area, or greater in two areas, such as speech or language, or occupational, or in academia could receive services. The pay scale for these services was determined by one's salary. They performed some evaluations on her. I shared that I was a special education teacher as well. I wanted them to know that I understood some of the methodologies and techniques that were discussed in terms of child development. When they determined after evaluating her that they recommended four days a week, at one hour a day of special education to begin with, I had reservations. I asked about receiving speech and occupational therapy. Initially, they expressed that she needed a developmental specialist. I thought to myself, "Was this the way the system worked? Why was it conceptualizing skills, and then when she's ready, we can proceed with language?!" It was generalizing concepts, and then foreseeing that language emerges. Sierra had a good understanding of pragmatics. This was a very composite and linear way of thinking. My intuition was telling me that Sierra needed help with communication from a variety of therapies. Building upon receptive and expressive language was essential. Having speech therapy simultaneously, with occupational therapy was critical in terms of her development.

Like the beginning of a horror movie, I was dismayed. I saw Sierra playing the role of this innocent victim. At the same time, she was a protagonist and hero. I didn't want to see other's as villains because of an antiquated system. I would be leaping through tall buildings ready to face what was presented to us. We were Wonder Woman and Wonder Girl. Sierra was the star in this. I created a team, one that extended, beyond the two of us. I took a snap shot of what it would look like in my mind. Then, proceeded to do research on the web for private speech therapists and occupational therapists.

Starting with Speech

After I called a couple of speech therapists, I had invited one over to interview. Loretta arrived at our home. She was friendly and outgoing. We directed her to the large playroom area. One of the first things I noticed was the profuseness of a strong scented perfume. It was a requirement of mine to have a therapist refrain from wearing this. Besides, children with special needs were often sensitive to chemicals. I hadn't wanted Sierra, nor myself to breathe this in. I decided to wait until after the session to discuss this with her, if in fact, it was a good fit.

I watched Loretta engage with Sierra. She exhibited a loud and boisterous tone. She over-exaggerated words, however she was very attentive upon working with her. She was forthright and humorous. The animal sounds she made, I found to be rather funny. Still, there was a rapid flow within the pacing of her movements. She asked many questions to Sierra, infrequently pausing, in between. In my anticipation for her to arrive at an impasse, where she would slow down, allowing for opportunities for Sierra to express more, it never occurred. I was questionable whether she felt comfortable with the silence, being aware and attentive to the gestures, sounds, or babbles and be able to join with her. Sierra moved about the room and was distracted by the overstimulation from external stimuli. It was eliciting more of a dysregulation, and a hypersensitivity.

After about a half hour of her working with Sierra, she gathered up her belongings. We said our goodbyes. As I scouted about the room, I searched for Sierra's handmade wooden stacker. It was nowhere to be found. I called Loretta and left a message inquiring about it. I indicated how much she loved this beautiful little stacker. It was a great educational toy for learning shapes, colors, sequencing, and building. Also, it was beneficial for imaginary and interactive play. We could use them in activities accentuating this back and forth reciprocity by rolling them, playing peek-a-boo with glasses over our eyes, for a hat, or creating rocks for a boat. It enhanced fine and gross motor skills by rolling and stacking them, stretching the legs to reach and grab, using the whole body including the pelvic area, arms, and legs, and fingers.

I reached out and contacted Loretta, again inquiring about it and that I would be amenable to picking it up. I hadn't heard back from her. I couldn't fathom not returning something that meant a lot to a child, one that was a valuable teaching tool for her. I hoped nothing serious happened with her. I suppose it wasn't the right fit. I tried to let it go. There were greater areas to focus on.

Kelly

Kelly was lovely—As she entered our home, she smiled brightly with a warm, hello. Respectfully, she asked where we would prefer her working with Sierra. I motioned to her, as I walked over to the sunlit room with large windows. She commented on the great space being quiet and serene, overlooking the water. Almost immediately, Sierra took a keen interest in her. She was articulate, exuberant and attentive. For the most part, Kelly followed Sierra's lead. She took out a couple of her own toys. One was of a colorful textured flap book. She maintained a nice easy momentum and exhibited inflexion in a soft, yet confident tone. She laughed along with Sierra, in a genuine way. Instinctively, I felt she was the right therapist. When Kelly left the house that morning, a greater hope was restored. I called her soon after, as I was excited for her to begin with us.

We agreed to her coming two days a week. Soon after, we discussed adding another day. Insurance allotted sixty visits of speech and occupational therapy annually, however, we knew that speech was critical for Sierra. We were determined to do whatever we could for Sierra, to reach her fullest potential. One that was unlimited in scope.

Kelly encouraged me to be a significant part of all the sessions. I was appreciative of this, as I was eager to learn anything and everything to support Sierra. Kelly and I developed a mutual respect and a liking towards each other. It was a complementary relationship. She was creative, and she valued my artistic background. She commented about how much she appreciated our natural toys. She encouraged me to use my skills, as in offering the applications and benefits of these toys, and various ways of using them in a blog. She was very motivating, and I looked forward to our sessions together. Kelly brought a variety of her own toys in a large bag, which Sierra enjoyed. One example was an Elefun toy, and several others with cause and effect, along with a variety of puzzles.

Typically, Sierra began with an animal puzzle. Kelly was very organized. She secured the pieces in a small plastic bag with a zip. This was also helpful in developing Sierra's fine motor skills, as Kelly would wait to see what Sierra would do. If Sierra waited or looked at her, Kelly would remain silent. Then, wide eyed and looking stumped, she would exaggerate this by opening up her arms asking, "What do you want?" Then, she would exaggerate, "Oh, you want the bag?" Sierra would reach out to take hold of it. Sierra would open the bag, as Kim said "O-p-e-n" with heightened affect with emphasis on the individual sounds. Sometimes, Sierra would dump them out on the floor. Together, they would turn them over. Kelly would continue to ask Sierra questions such as, "Where's the cow?" She would pause and give Sierra the opportunity to reflect, motor plan and think, before picking it up from the floor adjacent to the puzzle. Then, when Sierra placed it in the correct spot, she would happily say, "moo moo." She engaged with her, attentively. Sometimes, Sierra would imitate. Kelly's face lit up, as Sierra was enthusiastic in participating in a variety of activities. She would reach out to clutch them in her tiny hands vivaciously and attempt to make different sounds. Kelly used more of a floortime approach during these early days. Kelly would partake in a lot of songs and used nursery rhymes helping to elicit language. The stringing together of words with sound moved through the auditory and memory centers of the brain, in the hippocampus and frontal lobe, and could assist her in her communication. I was inspired by Kelly and Sierra, interacting and enjoying the engagement. It put a spark back in my life. Her gentle and animated way was contagious.

Kelly's ideas were well thought out in terms of her approach providing support. There was always a beginning, middle and an end. She would also integrate fine and gross motor within sessions, using vestibular and proprioceptive movement. She'd lay out an obstacle course with maybe, a tunnel and figures. She added in various colored or sized and textured balls or played peek-a-boo through the large open circles at each end. Sometimes, she set up bowling pins afterwards, and when Sierra even attempted it, she'd always respond with, "Good job, Sierra!!" When she did puzzles—nearing the end, she sang a familiar song every time, "Bye-bye cow, I'll see you on Thursday, "Bye-bye, horse, I'll see you on Thursday", "Bye-bye pig, I'll see you on Thursday." Kim let her know she would be returning, while providing her with a reinforcement of concepts.

What I found so helpful was her encouragement in me doing activities at home with Sierra. Artwork included finger painting, and cutting and pasting along with collages, as well. She created a picture book with words for Sierra. She divided it up into different sections with categories such as, "Favorite Toys, Foods we Eat, Bathroom, and Outings." Sierra had the opportunity to use this to enhance greater communication. She located the picture, made a choice, initiated, turned to me and showed me what she wanted. There was sequencing involved with movement with activities that aided in motor planning. By incorporating the utilization of visuals and auditory components, Sierra's strengths were capitalized upon.

Kelly was truly one of the best speech therapists. She was kind, supportive, and responsible. Although she shared with me that she was pregnant early on, we hired her. I knew she had a gift. It was well worth it. We appreciated the wide range of information she gave so freely, and all her effort and care. After nine months of working with us, she took a leave of absence for a couple of months. She was confident she would be returning. Still, we had to find someone in that period of time. Sierra was about two and a few months of age. We decided to hire a speech therapist to complement her, to capitalize and expand upon what was working effectively, for Sierra's needs.

Melony

Melony was quite progressive in the field as a speech and language pathologist. She had a background in sensory integration challenges and shared she had attended many workshops in this area. She was also a trained hippo-therapist and rode horses much of her life. She had a good understanding of the body and a repertoire of other skills. Trained in PROMPT therapy (an acronym for Prompts for Restructuring Oral Muscular Phonetic Targets) for many years and with several certifications. "The technique is a tactile-kinesthetic approach that uses touch cues to a patient's articulators (jaw, tongue, lips) to manually guide them through a targeted word, phrase or sentence" (The PROMPT Institute). It was a no brainer for me to hire her as her therapist. We started with Melody shortly after Kelly. We knew Kelly would be soon taking a leave of absence due to her giving birth, and for a short time used both of their services.

We figured it would be great to explore hippotherapy at the farm Melony conducted sessions at. Hippotherapy was the use of horseback riding as a therapeutic or rehabilitative treatment, especially as a means of improving coordination, balance, and strength. It aided many different populations. Cerebral palsy and other neurological disorders, such as autism were assisted through this approach. Melody used her background as an avid rider of horses, and training in hippotherapy, along with her skills as a speech therapist to help people. There were also occupational therapists available to work with children there.

Sierra's first day of going to the farm to ride was a memorable one. She was just two years of age. It was springtime. It was about twenty-five minutes away from us. Traveling along this scenic route, through windy roads, though with a variety of beautiful trees, and around a reservoir was lovely. We pulled up past a wooden gate where some horses grazed. Just as you parked your car into the lot, from around the bend, across the unpaved area were some barnyard stalls. The horse's names were etched in them. I pointed out a couple of them to Sierra to familiarize her with them, and aid in the excitement. Melony came out to greet us, and we walked into the indoor barn. We watched a couple of other children coral around with support from a volunteer. She introduced us to the welcoming volunteer. We went into the outdoor riding stable where Melony quickly went over a grabbed a small bicycle helmet for Sierra, as the others were too large for her tiny head. Sierra looked around, wide eyed and curious. She cringed her nose a bit, as she took in the pungent smells of the farm. There were a lot of horses, maybe twelve or so, pigs roaming, as well as chickens and ducks around the bend. You could see them as Sierra rode up into the woods that had clear paths.

When it was Sierra's turn, Melony assisted her lifting her high up on Dude. Dude was beautiful, sleek, and dark chocolate brown in color. He was the first horse she had ever rode. I was so excited for her to experience this, although admittedly, I was a little nervous. Sierra was hesitant to giddy up on him. Yet, with encouragement and support, she made her way up on the saddle. I walked alongside Sierra down and around the farm. I was impressed by Sierra's courage. Melony's positivity was contagious, as she joyfully pointed out several of the animals while they galloped along. She stopped at certain intervals, holding up pictures of different material. Some were contained on cards, while others were trinkets of animals or other objects. She asked Sierra questions providing choices for her, as she held up two items of something, as to where she liked to go, what animals she'd like to see, etc. She reinforced what Sierra picked, by enunciating it with varied intonations.

We alternated between going to Melony's office once a week, sometimes twice and one day at the farm. Our sessions were consistent over the course of the next two years. During hippotherapy, Sierra often approximated words and at times enunciate three syllable words while on the horse. The input of the horse was wonderful in aiding vestibular and proprioceptive movement, as well. Melony had such a passion for it and an adoration for horses. She was attentive and engaging with Sierra throughout the half hour sessions. We were in good hands.

Occupational Therapy

Movement in a rhythmic motion was a priority for self-discovery, learning, and integration, and for enhancing the body-mind connection. With the underlying principles of engagement through play, language would hopefully, emerge and sounds would become more viable and fluid. When repetition through rote representation was encouraged without more attention to a global perspective, information could be lost, as it wouldn't prove to be valuable. Enjoyment was a factor in sustainability of concepts. When children's brains were more pliable and receptive, this was the best time for them to retain information. Sierra began occupational therapy at nineteen months old.

A social-emotional approach with back and forth reciprocity where the child is engaged in the activity because of an interest in it, builds upon trust. It also aids in self-regulation and organization of the mind-body connection. Occupational therapy was a wonderful approach where one incorporates movement with play. This enhances not only fine and gross motor skills, but vestibular and proprioceptive input. In addition, it promotes areas of brain development which improves receptive and expressive language. It has the capacity to build upon concrete to abstract thinking.

We searched for an occupational therapist nearby. We were allotted sixty visits per year combined with speech therapy through our insurance. We found a therapist at a center affiliated with a local hospital. We made an appointment to go there. First, we had to receive an O.T. evaluation. This encompassed a variety of skill taking. Micky, the occupational therapist, used an approach that took into account her physical, social, emotional, sensory and cognitive abilities. Micky recommended her coming once a week. We made morning appointments and were consistent in arriving on time for the sessions.

As soon as we got there, we were warmly greeted by the secretary, as I signed Sierra's name. I'd arrive there a little early. I'd take out one of Sierra's favorite snacks-blueberries. She gobbled them down as she picked up a book on the table adjacent to where we sat. Soon after our therapist, Ms. Micky came out. She called out, "Ms. Siiieeerra" enthusiastically, with a broad toothy smile. We were led down the hallway, as she took Sierra's lead into a relatively small, square shaped room.

The space had a climbing wall with a rope, swing, and large colorful mats. She used a variety of techniques and toys. Micky would also include a variety of sensory input, such as play-do and thera-putty. Colored tubes with ridges to push and pull apart, as well as cause and effect toys were available to Sierra. She had a caring nature, was attentive to her and challenged her. Micky was thoughtful and direct in her approach. She structured certain activities though, offered choices. She was articulate and quick-witted and used songs and nursery rhymes to engage Sierra. Sierra formed a nice relationship with her. She laughed with Micky, especially during the time she sang to Sierra on the flat swing. I believe she enjoyed this the most. The forty-five minutes were productive. I remained present in the room and participated at times. Micky had built a nice rapport with Sierra.

As the sessions progressed, I inquired about adding another day. Micky expressed that Sierra was one of those kids who benefitted from occupational therapy every day. She prefaced this by referring to her as being one of those sensory kids. My immediate response was to add another day. She hesitated, as she needed to look at her schedule. I assumed this was more about being booked with other children and having no slots open. She had limited availability and encouraged me to do activities at home. She shared that when and if another slot opened up, she would contact me.

Determined to do whatever I could during these critical years of Sierra's life, I purchased almost everything imaginable, and anything I believed could benefit Sierra. We even went as far as getting an itinerant swing. I was so excited about it, however although the swing was a little hard to assemble. It was heavy with large parts. With our ceilings being kind of low, just barely fit the structure. It just about fit into our living-playroom area. We used it ten times, at most.

We continued attending sessions with Micky once a week for about six months. I didn't see huge progress, maybe because it was only once a week. We were optimistic about finding a place she could attend at least two or three times a week. We continued our search.

We found a place in the northern suburbs of New York, close to the border of our town. It was about twenty minutes away. It was held in a one-story newer brick building. The occupational therapist invited me in to meet her prior to beginning with her. She expressed wanting to know more about Sierra and to see if it would be a good fit. I really appreciated this.

The office was a large clean space, filled with all sorts of sensory-motor supplies. The occupational therapist shared she had just recently left her job at a school district to start her own practice. This was a brand-new office. We were excited to come. It was bright and functionally savvy. Sierra had more room to move about and explore. She had set up circuits for Sierra. She loved jumping from the large mats, doing somersaults, crawling through the tunnel, throwing a ball from above, and dipping into the ball pit. We tried doing a type of listening therapy to improve speech. This included a variety of sounds being heard to help with regulating areas of the body balancing wavelengths and for restoration of it. It aided in calming, integrating and also in receptive and self-expression. This required placing headphones on the ears every day for at least two weeks at a time, for it to have a greater effect. Shortly after Sierra put the headset on, she took it off. We tried this a few times. I figured we could try it out, again soon. After a few months of coming, she had closed her office. We were disappointed, as we genuinely liked her. We saw some positive changes happening for Sierra.

Further Exploration

There were things I needed to explore regarding a more in depth understanding of Sierra's development. Discovering more of the scope of Sierra's issues was essential. I found myself in a lonely place, in a quantifiably desperate attempt to obtain real answers from a skilled doctor providing me with some sort of clarity. Hesitantly, I dialed THAT number. The number of the developmental pediatrician on that little slip of paper I held onto, as was given to us by our pediatrician. Dr. Chen assured us we'd get an appointment quickly as she was a comrade of hers, and she had worked in that hospital. She expressed concern for Sierra emphasizing that she wanted her to receive all the support she needed. We were appreciative of her willingness to help us and her giving nature. Our appointment arrived in about six weeks.

Developmental Spiral

The stark white walls and sterile appearance, along with the disinfectant smell that permeated through it, as we walked through the corridors of the hospital evoked a jitteriness within me. I reminded myself, that we were in a hospital. The stifling environment and our reason for being here, heightened all my senses. I tried to focus on the positive. There were some colorful pictures, a playroom for children, and books in the waiting room. Still, I would do almost anything not to be there. As we waited, I noticed my husband's raised brow line, and furrowed look upon his face. His pale tones and a worried look had become more apparent.

"Sierra Schwartz", echoed from across the waiting room area. We were led into a stark white office. As I looked around, I noticed a sparse quality, with one picture hanging up on the wall. The doctor was friendly with a welcoming smile. She appeared in her mid-fifties, so I gathered that she had some experience and knowledge on the subject matter. She spoke to us for about a good half an hour taking history of Sierra's birth, symptoms, milestones, etc. She had a small table with some old blocks placed upon it, along with white paper with peeled and half used crayons.

The doctor asked Sierra to sit down at an old wooden desk. She handed Sierra a piece of paper with somewhat faded black and white drawings on it. It was divided into four pictures. One was of a dog, another of a cat, another of a child, and one other of a house. She asked her to identify the pictures. I thought, maybe if I had a magnifying glass, I could make some of these pictures out. It looked like an old worn-out photocopy. The pictures were sketchy with faded black ink. She asked Sierra to point to the animals, as she said their names. I wondered why she gave her something like this. Why expect a child to point to the correct picture that appeared nothing like reality! Sierra got a couple of them right. She asked her to build with the blocks. Sierra stacked a few of them. Typically, she stacked ten or more. She asked her to identify colors on the blocks. Then, prompted her to count them. Sierra was able to articulate some of this, but the words were unclear. Then, she nonchalantly stated, "PDD-Autism" (Pervasive Developmental Disorder). I was somewhat taken aback by her analysis, but not so much surprised with the method she used to determine this. I snickered inside at the methodology she used in conducting this evaluation. I thought, perhaps to some degree, Sierra may have a progressive learning disorder and neurological challenges that were caused by autoimmune issues. However, I reminded myself that she was a developmental pediatrician and not an immunologist or a neurologist. Developmental pediatrics is a medical specialty that focuses on the evaluation, diagnosis, treatment, and ongoing care of children who are experiencing developmental delays and/ or behavioral or educational difficulties.

It was encouraged by the doctor to explore various options. She informed us about a preschool program as part of a Jewish

Community Center. She said it had been around for several years and heard great things about it. That could be something promising, however it was a bit far from our home, over an hour away.

The doctor eluded to Aspen Trails being our best bet. It was an ABA (Applied Behavioral Analysis) program. "ABA is a method of therapy used to improve or change specific behaviors. In simple terms, ABA changes the environment in order to change the behavior" (ABA Degree Programs). It helps to develop new skills, shape and refine previously learned skills and decrease socially significant problem behaviors. It is a system of rewards and consequences.

The doctor concluded that it was a reputable place with a highly trained staff. Although being skilled in the technique they offered was essential, I wanted an approach that if necessary, would be modified to meet Sierra's individualized needs. I hoped to work with whomever we chose as a team. These people would have to gain Sierra's trust.

The developmental pediatrician saw Sierra for a glimpse of time. There were more answers to this puzzle. The metaphor of being a round peg in a square world, was glaring at me. I was determined to continue my quest for understanding more, exploring options, and gaining anecdotes from parents about their experiences.

Aspen Trails

A spen Trails, a rather lovely name for a company. It made me ponder about the trees, nature, and the forest. If only I could find the right program that was more inclined to be outdoors and in nature. That day I was at the park with Sierra, watching her sift through the tiny granules in the sand box. It warmed my heart watching her explore.

After a little while, a woman from Aspen Trails returned my call. She shared, "We'll have to put you on a waiting list."

"How long of a wait will that be?" I asked.

"It's hard to say. There are multiple therapists and children starting, while others are moving on."

Perhaps, this wasn't the best fit. However, if they were in such high demand, something might be very beneficial about this program. Besides, all there seemed to be in these programs was ABA. My stomach felt like an upside-down hot apple pie with drippings stuck to its sides. My head was immersed with questions about this approach and whether to pursue this further. Time was ticking. Reluctantly, I said, "Sure, put my name on the list."

I concluded that since we had been given a referral about this agency from the developmental pediatrician, as well as, from a well-respected man from our community that perhaps, this could help our daughter. The man who shared this had led parent groups. He said that this program transformed his daughter at a very young age, and that she was recovered from any autistic tendencies. He informed me that she was the most social child in his family. He commented on how it was a rigorous program, however worth making the sacrifice. There were many hours invested which affected sleep with little time, if any to participate in other activities. He concluded that they were dedicated and very organized in their approach. It was one of a very limited number of methodologies which insurance covered.

Six weeks later we received a phone call from Maria, the supervisor from Aspen Trails. She said that a slot for Sierra had opened up. We would need to commit to twenty hours a week, and no less. Otherwise, there was a chance the therapy may not be effective enough to make lasting changes, as it had been studied and proven. I felt desperate to help our daughter and in anticipation agreed to have them come. Even though it didn't seem right in my gut, I would at least commit to something that was tried and proven.

The first day arrived. Three women along with a supervisor came to our home. Very professional, notebooks in hand with charts and goals ready to be delved into, to measure gains. I must admit, I was somewhat uncomfortable with this type of regimented format, with discrete trials containing repetition of concepts across a range of topics, in linear form. Sierra had to be tested to determine what level she was at, in terms of comprehension and receptive and expressive language.

Still, the extinguish, reward, punishment emphasis wasn't something that sat well with me. The supervisor shared that she understood about a more natural way of working with Sierra, using these principals. I felt comforted by that.

It was a lot of hours to commit to, at twenty hours a week. I reminded myself that just maybe-maybe, more was better. "Okeee", I thought. In my gut, there was a nudging sensation to take caution. This was all so new to me, and I was trying to really make sense, as to what would work best. Sierra was so young at two years and four months old. I was concerned about her naptime. They agreed to reduce the hours to eighteen and a half per week since Sierra had hippotherapy one day, which they said was of importance. It wasn't much, but at least they were amenable to this.

The therapists shared their large black manuals with me. It contained lots of pages for collecting data and areas to chart goals to input information from discrete trials. I tried to understand how this was going to enhance verbal communication, being that she had global apraxia. Perhaps, there was something I was missing. Maybe, the therapists would help Sierra in such a way, that their personalities would enhance the meaning of the tasks given, if they were fun and interesting to her.

There was nothing wrong in trying a quantified approach that had been heavily researched. I got on the bandwagon to join what was "proven" by state standards.

How I missed the simple life, before all of this happened. I had to face it, all of the heaviness. Was I was going to be a part of the conglomeration of those who worked within the premise of ABA? Perhaps, most of the country was more left brained, which was why this was the only approach insurance covered and schools adhered to.

My husband thought it was beneficial to place cameras in the three rooms that the therapists worked with Sierra. I would have access to viewing whatever skills they were teaching that I could support her with. At the three-week mark, I found some things unsettling. There were several factors, I had questioned. I was discouraged from being in the room. I was her mother, the most important role model in her life. It was essential in those early years to have mommy or daddy present, to work together in a way that was built upon trust. I was in the house and so, I agreed to what their protocol was.

The next day arrived. I watched closely, and more intently into the camera. I squinted my eyes further and tried to make sense of what had presented itself on the screen. The therapist pointed to Sierra's little orange chair and in a stern monotone voice said, "Sit Down." When Sierra hadn't responded immediately, she repeated herself, again, delegating to her to, sit down. She wanted her to sit in a chair for fifteen minutes. I couldn't believe it! She was only two years old. I rushed into the room and expressed to her in as composed a manner, as I could, that this was not okay. I asked her if she would leave. It was utter nonsense to place this demand on another, let alone a young innocent child. Immediately, I called the supervisor, Maria. She agreed it was too long of a stretch of time to request this, for a child of Sierra's age. She encouraged me to give her a chance, following up with speaking to her about this. I was not in favor of it.

A couple of weeks later, Sierra and I were circling around our neighborhood in her little red wagon. As I pulled her on the sidewalk, we sang songs, and pointed out sights and sounds. All of a sudden, I observed something that made my heart sink. She tugged at her hair, removing strands of it. She had never done this before. Something was definitely wrong. She must have been so stressed.

The next day, I reached out to Aspen Trails. Again, I asked for the supervisor. I spoke with her calmly and directly. I did my best to maintain a state of grace, as it was important to me that we had a congenial relationship. I asked Maria if the therapist could be switched to one that was more suited to Sierra's needs. I explained to her that during her time in our home she appeared disinterested, and was somewhat, aloof and unenthusiastic. The therapist refrained from hugging or out showing any affection. I continued that it was not supporting Sierra well, and that she benefitted from a more natural approach.

The supervisor came for a visit. Concerned, she sat down with me to figure out the most effective way to move forward. Maria confessed that ABA was not working as well as she would have liked to meet Sierra's needs. She continued with stating that she believed if it was done more naturally, it would have proved to be more effective. She commented that Sierra was atypical for a child with traits of "autism". She commented that she was affectionate, social, and understood a wide range of topics. Maria commented on her vast potential, including her overall intelligence. I sensed that she was the most adept at working with Sierra. Yet, she wouldn't be able to work with her, as her position was primarily, in overseeing the therapists. Maria exhibited to us that she was trained in utilizing a naturalistic teaching method that would have served Sierra more effectively, and that the other therapists were not trained in this way. Her recommendation was speech and occupational therapy at five days a week, each. She reinforced that Sierra was unique, and that in her six years of working with children there was only one other child she thought ABA wasn't the best fit for. I was grateful for Maria's openness in expressing this, especially since this was her area of expertise. I appreciated her perception, insight and willingness to share with us this information.

It would be a huge expense to hire a speech therapist and occupational therapist at the amount of days suggested. Insurance would not cover this. Insurance had not yet, reimbursed us for their duration, in our home. This was attributed to Applied Behavioral Analysis listed under an inappropriate code, allotted for those under the influence of drug and alcohol. Our insurance company stated they were not going to change their coding. My husband had been on the phone with the insurance company every day for six months, at least an hour a day. Because of his relentlessness and determination, he was able to land a spot on the national news. Because of his tenacity and passion in fighting for the rights of our daughter, it assisted many others receiving this methodology, as the codes were changed. To this day, we are still waiting for the state to review our records for reimbursement. It's considered a class action lawsuit.

Over the span of the next several days, I thought long and hard about what our next steps would be. I continued to work with Sierra. After having therapists in our home for six weeks at twenty plus hours a week, we were reestablishing a new momentum, having a more relaxed atmosphere. We were finding more positive outlets to recover from a stressful time into a more forgiving space.

Standing Up or
Sitting Down

I was not going to allow Sierra's diagnosis to hold her back. There was more than one methodology to be utilized in our schools for children with neurological issues, including autism. Applied Behavioral Analysis was a proponent of a reward, consequences approach. If you perform this task, you will receive a tangible object, as a reward. I wondered what the incentive was to do task analysis for children who had social-emotional challenges. Placing value on the connectedness of the child, as an individual through play, the cornerstone for learning would prove to be more effective in wanting to interact. This was not because of a reward, but because of the simple enjoyment of the process itself. Building upon simple to complex skills would be more innately, driven. We were social beings that valued interrelationships, as in being drawn to the attention, as in the connectedness found in each other through empathy, thereby furthering language development.

Capitalizing on one's inner strengths using a back and forth dialogue, with subtle "oohs" and "ahhs" and "over here" and "over there", and by opening and closing circles of interest to the child made much more sense to me. The opening and closing of circles is a technique utilized in a methodology called DIR Floortime®. (Developmental, Individual-differences and Relationship-based model) "It was developed by Dr. Stanley Greenspan to provide a foundational framework for understanding human development" (ICDL). For example; if a child reaches out, with a look, he opens the circle. When a parent responds by looking back, he builds on the child's action. When the child in turn responds to the parent, by smiling, vocalizing, reaching, or turning away, he is closing the circle. If a parent responds to the child's response by holding out a toy by saying, "Do you want to play?" By echoing the child's vocalization and the child responds with another gesture, a look, a smile, or hand movement, they have opened and closed another circle. Fairly, quickly the baby learns from this experience, that he can cause mommy and daddy to react, but also cause and effect from toys. He learns he has an impact on the world. It is essential for all human interaction.

In acknowledging one's interests, building rapport, while offering challenging scenarios, that is where the greatest learning happens, as we assimilate existing information with new information. Bringing in one or two dolls or toys to engage with a child, with affect following the child's movements goes a long way. All the while, taking into consideration developmental challenges and understanding them from a social emotional standpoint was critical. Here, receptive language has the plausibility to increase, and this can expand to more expressive language. With a cartoon character such as Elmo, a shy child can emerge from a more introverted state into a more extroverted one. The reward was seen and acknowledged through the exploration of one's self and his environment, by interaction of reciprocity with oneself and another, and concrete can lead to more abstract concepts.

The ABA system was designed many decades ago and prior to this was called, behavior modification. ABA replaced this term because the latter approach suggested attempting to change the behavior without clarifying relevant behavior-environment interactions. It was also initially created in the 1960's for children having issues more severe in scope. However, the wide range of children who have "autism" can and do have the capacity to socialize and also learn by application in a more humane and natural way.

What is autism? It is a developmental and neurological disorder. Where does it come from? Toxic exposures and mutations in genes. A variety of reasons. There are abnormalities in the brain structure or function. The children labeled with attention-deficit disorder back in the nineteen nineties now, had symptoms more severe in the current year of our two thousand millennium babies. WHY? We had to ask ourselves.

It is essential to heal our bodies in conjunction with learning. If a child is hitting their head on the floor—most likely, they are not feeling well. They are suffering from brain inflammation. It's a sickness stemming from the entire nervous system and affecting many other areas within the body. There is not a one size fits all approach. However, we cannot leave any stone unturned. We have to navigate through our own systems, and the way we process material from a holistic perspective. Healing the body, mind, and spirit was the most effective way of reversing the incongruencies in our children's systems. What we needed were trained doctors from various fields that worked in collaboration to find answers from a biomedical, psychological and educational perspective. Our children will become adults. The numbers of special needs children were dramatically increasing. Here is where the clock mattered.

It was our duty as concerned members of society to do more research and speak out—As parents of children we are here to teach ourselves and one another, and to be empathic to the unique needs and perspectives of each individual. The reward is in the interaction of helping and supporting one another.

Dr. Kapone

We were off to see the wizard, the Wonderful Wizard of Oz. I had hoped for this, even if it were under the guise of a neurologist. In whatever shape or form, I was ready to obtain more information to help us on this path. I had heard about Dr. Kapone from a woman I met at the horse farm where Sierra participated in hippo-therapy. She was the mother of two children, one who had auditory processing disorder and language challenges and the other having, a rare bone disorder. It was this child, that she found out something startling. She found out that her son was going to live a long life, after another "skilled" doctor told her otherwise, cutting his life in half, maybe if he lived that long. Dr. Kapone seemed to have been more skilled. The mom shared he was more logical, definitive and refined in his determinations. She commented on his warmth and friendliness, and how he'd get down on the floor with the kids, as if he weren't afraid to act like a human being, even with his doctor coat on. I made an appointment about six months out because the receptionist let us know his schedule was full. We would wait.

After forty-five minutes of driving, we had arrived. Andy, Sierra, and I walked into a low story brick building, and through a couple of short corridors. Sierra enjoyed pressing the buttons in the elevator. Soon after, we walked into their office. It felt inviting. There was a round table with crayons, paper and some children's books. We assisted Sierra with her coat and she quickly sat down to color. She soon got up. Andy and she went into another vacant room with some large gross motor toys, one was a large structure containing large beads to slide across and back again. This was seen at many pediatric offices. Soon after, we were called in.

Dr. Kapone had an engaging smile and was charming, with a likeable way about him. He was tall, dark rimmed glasses, and a warm smile. He appeared more like an actor, than a doctor. He had an endearing way, which worked well for children. Sierra moved about the room. She gravitated towards the extra-large treasure box where blocks and other figures were in. Sierra grabbed some and played for a short while with them. She looked up at Dr. Kapone in brief moments, as she swiveled about. At one point, he sat down on the floor with us, as we answered some pertinent questions asked by him. He was friendly and engaging with Sierra.

He checked Sierra's head circumference, eye tracking, and some other visual special components. He asked her some questions. One of them was her dog's name. We had previously shared she had a dog named, Maggie.

Dr. Kapone observed and analyzed Sierra's overall development. Her diagnoses were global dyspraxia (ideomotor based), sensory integration disorder, hypotonia and akathisia. He stated that she didn't have autism. She was social and engaged. Based on other diagnostic tests, he stated that her significant communication challenges were affected by the sensory component. Integration was key. He recommended a movement-based, language-immersed program as appropriate for Sierra. When we asked about schools or programs, he didn't have any more information about them, in terms of their specifics. We were very appreciative of his knowledge and advice. He recommended us returning in a year, when Sierra would be four years of age.

Forging Ahead Through the Artistry of Life

The fluidity of colors on a tangible surface could cathartically transform areas in my life that needed to be tended to and released. My friend, the canvas, offered some relief. Use of space, line, color, brush stroke, uniformity, and balance were all part of this collective unconscious or integrated whole. Something Carl Jung spoke about, especially with regard to, the creation of a mandala to witness the subconscious whole, as in dream states and overall analysis. Through the creation of art, I was a witness to my own observations. It was something I had control over. This served as my "go to place" or "happy place". It was a subliminal force assisting me in interpreting and analyzing areas of my life. It was helpful for self-actualizing. I gathered information from my paintings.

Something I had become more aware of; The bright colors I layered from a more positive space and those that were more complementary towards each other, sometimes gave into a spectrum that contained hues that represented self-doubt. I held that brush in hand, where I could turn beauty into a hodge-podge of stormy colors. I washed over some up the lively colors, I applied in some of my work. Yet, when I utilized more controlled mediums, my creations were often, more forgiving with mediums such as pencil, pen and ink, or with oils or soft pastels. I enjoyed being more fluid, as there was a freedom involved. Chaos would unfold. I was driven to look further within, into those places, that weren't so perfect, or were they? To be perfectly, imperfect. That was key; placing acceptance on my value, and self-worth, what I was destined to contribute to myself, and to this world.

In my thirties, I wrote children's stories adjoining my two greatest passions; art and writing. This turned into illustrations. The first ones were a series of angels. Their unique characters spoke to me. I picked them up one by one, transforming them into a story called, "A Princess, Am I?" It was about finding one's true essence. Through meeting significant others, as in aspects of ourselves, the messages were restored within us, to elicit the gifts we came here for. Writing stories was a safe and honest way for self-reflection and growth, offering a tangible way of self-expression.

As I sat in a different space, I experienced life not only through my eyes, but through my daughter's. In a very instrumentally humble way, I was learning so much about myself through her. In terms of her use of applying color, as well as in cutting and pasting, I watched both the joy and the frustration of it. That stop and go method was being somewhat ingrained in her. It was imperative to unravel it. Life was more superfluous then that. To disturb the movement in one's natural capacity to flow was like a jolt to the body, depleting the body of its understanding of its own innate potential. It was time to fuel up.

I continued encouraging Sierra by acknowledging and fostering a creativity she held while I instilled within her a freedom of expression. This allowed for greater fluidity, cohesiveness, and integration, among other benefits. I stepped away and back again, and watched the artist explore, within. I noticed a dichotomy between two forces—The happiness emanating from the idea where she was simply enjoying the process, and the frustration in the struggle to produce something more. An example was when cutting was harder for her beyond the straight forward lines. Another difficulty was in creating a more formal image. I assisted Sierra in circular movements in cutting. When she stopped, I presented other materials saying, "wow" or "ooh", or "great", with greater affect and interest. I might hand Sierra one of the pictures she cut and ask her if she wanted the glue. Sierra did much of the placement and pasting. The back and forth reciprocity and dialogue was helpful in building greater trust in ourselves and in the quality of what we produced together as mother and daughter. It was the beauty of the experience, not the quantification of what was manifested or developmentally appropriate.

Sierra explored materials at her own pace. Slowing down and breaking things into smaller increments was helpful, to not overwhelm her. Listening with intent was essential. When she was reluctant in utilizing her wrists to turn the picture over, as it was challenging for her, we would take a pause. In between these intervals, we wiggled our bodies out, especially our arms and our wrists, and begin again. There was no right or wrong way. All was unfolding as part of the experience. I asked some open-ended questions, as I watched her body and facial expressions. She led the way. I'd say simple phrases like, "ooh, pretty", or "here you go", while encouraging her to make decisions. "Where's the glue?" "Hmm, is it over there?" I might ask, "Wait a minute" and with affect ask, "Where are you going?" "Oh, okay, over there." If Sierra needed to reacclimate, we would return later. I would leave whatever we were working on out, possibly resume later, or perhaps, I brought it closer to her. These were all a part of creating circles. As she assimilated information from subtle cues, an awareness within the body occurred. Her proprioceptive and vestibular system was reacclimating in terms of building awareness and interest, allowing in more information, and integrating concepts building upon the simple to more complex.

I would shrug my shoulders with my arms and hands out asking, "What's next?" Sometimes, I assisted a little more. Other times, less. Each stroke or movement was beautiful, whatever the final product was. It was in the process unfolding that served as a powerful reminder of the picture-perfect life.

Since Sierra enjoyed books so much, we incorporated them into works of art. Books that were "loved too much" where some were ripped and torn apart, we sometimes, recycled. We applied them on a canvas surface with different themes. One called "One Love". It was inspired by a Bob Marley book. Life was a series of images coming together, even when it seemed they were coming apart. Like a story with a beginning, middle and an end, this was occurring in the sequencing of making art.

As inductive thinkers there was an expansion in building upon concepts. This was opposed to deductive thinkers where a concept was broken down into its smallest components. If we took a picture, we'd see the branches, then the vastness of it and its greenery, and how it expands and moves upwards towards the sky. A deductive thinker might have seen the tree, the leaves, the branches, and the roots held in the soil in the ground.

Our journey here was special and unique according to the awakening of our ability to function and to grow. Life was not so cut and dry. More positive long-term results came from honoring where we were at, on our own time lines. We, as mentors for our children needed to nurture these places by acknowledging our own imperfections and challenges. To provide a safe environment where trust could be gained.

A nail was not to be driven into a piece of wood before the frame was prepared. That wooden frame could not be placed on before the process of creating that picture was completed. Every movement in itself, was an achievement. The earth was full of uneven surfaces and was not to be determined by another's frame of reference, as in not being good enough. Otherwise, the result is premature advancement, as in the simplicity of a frame hammered together, all too soon.

After ABA and Back Again

Sierra was home with me. I would continue with all I could to support her growth process. I was intuitive, and creative, and had a background in child development. I reminded myself that I was her mother. I would never give up on my child.

Our house overlooked a small lake. We could hear the sounds of the waterfall spilling into it from our kitchen. It provided a calm and serene atmosphere, especially during those morning hours. Eating breakfast in our little nook, was a satisfying experience, as you could hear the sounds of it. As the days and months passed, I became immersed into a place where the tranquility was diminishing. As I awoke, it became harder to get up. I remained in a cocoon like state, my feet propelled upwards, knees tucked beneath me coveted in a soft blanket. I tried to work through the intrepid feelings, not knowing if the day would bring more fulfillment in my daughter's life. I reminded myself that Sierra had her whole life ahead of her. Whatever I encountered could add greater fulfillment to her days, and whatever I chose to share in with her, was enough.

Our days together were filled with art and music classes, including Music for Aardvarks, The Little Gym, along with speech and occupational therapy. This provided her with a variety of supports so that Sierra could reach her fullest potential. I made decisions based upon what I felt would optimally provide her with what she needed. My husband was persistent in his declaration in stating she needed more. "More is better", he would adamantly, say. I wondered if his paradigm emphasized this, as he had severe dyslexia and he learned how to read when he was fifteen years of age. It was through repetition with an Orton Gillingham method, utilizing many modalities like hearing the words, writing them, saying them aloud, and repeating. After two summers in a well renowned school for Dyslexia, he learned how to read. It was quite miraculous and showed what could happen with proper dedication and support. Sierra would beat to the sound of her own drum.

At times, I flashed back to when I allowed those shots to be injected into her tiny body. It was like a sand trail that followed me. If only I could erase the tracks, and begin, again. Perhaps, I could.

Tell Your Story,
Not Mine

I yearned to hear her sweet little voice, one that was larger than life. By listening in on the subtleties of her movements and words, I noticed her eyes and face light up more, her inquisitive and imaginative nature being stirred. With giggles and belly laughs, or in the silence there was a voice inside longing to be reckoned with! Connections were being made in her circuitry, as synapses were being stimulated, as she moved to the beat of her own drum to continue to integrate more.

Even though we were warned about excess stimuli being emitted from electronics, there were benefits to them, as well. Sierra intently gravitated to those Baby Einstein videos she so loved. I reminded myself it was okay, sometimes. When the "oh no's" set in, as I looked at those colorful noisy objects moving across the screen, I would ask myself, "What if she looked at them for too long?" "Would she distance herself further from reality into an "autistic" type of world?"

I focused on supporting Sierra's strengths and struggles. Despite having severe apraxia challenges, motor planning issues in her oral motor cavity and her body, and vestibular and proprioceptive challenges, she was so innately, intelligent. "Mama" she would articulate at times. "Dada" was easier. Other words subsided. I hadn't known if they would pop up again, and sometimes had, infrequently.

One day, Sierra's speech therapist, Melanie, told me something that really threw me for a loop. When Sierra was just two and a half years of age she shared, "Words aren't going to come easy for her." It was as though my whole body went numb. My heart sank in disbelief in her audacity to even say such a thing. How could she know that? She hadn't been, even three years old. This was such brash judgement. Like those doctors with one size fits' all theories justifying complicated cases by putting a number on it, based upon some evidence from a random sample of people. It was like giving me false information, as if we had six more months to live! Did she have the professional reliability to say that? Making a statement like that without further knowledge was incredibly, insensitive. The next time we saw Melanie she apologized to us. She was heartfelt and expressed that it was unfair as she could not predict Sierra's future. She said it was her experience in working with children with receptive and expressive challenges, that she arrived at that conclusion. Although I accepted her apology, it was difficult, as this was my precious child and she was so young, and still, developing.

Sierra was a bright, capable human being, having so much potential. I prayed those pictures she showed me from a young age would someday turn into expressive language. I could relate to Sierra's way of viewing things, as I was a visual learner. The events of a whole story were seen in moving pictures, like I was watching a movie.

A Bigger Picture

At a recent yoga class during shavasana; The quiet more meditative part at the end of class where we laid down upon our mats, where all our hard work from doing the postures came to fruition. A few minutes after that, when we were ready, we were encouraged to place our feet upon the mat.

I laid in a swaddled state on my right side (representing a nurturing of our past, as in being a child) upon my yoga mat. The instructor shared, "Let this chapter of your life be whatever it is and know that this chapter can change." You can turn the page to something that will uplift you, enlighten you, and possibly, even change the course of your life. You don't have to stay in the past. It is exactly that. You have the power and the ability to change that. You can return to the mat again to close a chapter and open another chapter of your life." These words held such meaning for me. There is a beginning, middle, and an end in every day. A new chapter within the whole of the story that we were weaving constantly, throughout our lives. Like the meditation I led way back at Kripalu; Life comes full circle.

I continued taking Sierra outside in nature in open fields, often to the playground neighboring our town. Much of the time, there were few people who congregated there during the mornings. Sometimes, the nannies of young children were present, and although we spoke different languages, I enjoyed interacting with others, always while sharing and learning. I appreciated differences across all cultures.

As I pulled up to the parking lot nearest the playground, Sierra would immediately mitigate towards the fence. With an outstretched arm, she pressed her tiny hands against it, as she maneuvered her fingers upon the triangular orifices of the fence that separated the lot from the baseball field. Sometimes, she ran with me in the fields as I took her hand or allowed her to be in her own space. I sang to her a variety of songs from Music Together, Music for Aardvarks or repeated some whimsical nursery rhymes. I would experience some engagement from her. She'd laugh a little, yet I yearned to see more excitement seen in her affective states. I was happy she enjoyed some of the simple things like the swings, the slides and the little tunnel.

I tried not to let that nagging underlying sadness encompass me. A mother's yearning to hear their child express themselves, freely. I'd see other children communicating, initiating their wants with "No, Mommy." "I want to go there." "Watch me mommy." "Play with Me". I longed to hear those words. Sierra ran over to the swings and I would place her inside. I sang to her. I would pause in between, going slow at times, giving space for any response to request, to reach or point, to show me something. Watching for those subtle cues to expand on, as in any imitation of sounds or movements she formed. I gave her choices encouraging any type of response. Sometimes it was with yes or no questions, like—"Do you want to go on the swing or slide? If there wasn't any verbal response, I might ask, "Can you show me?" If she wanted to leave, as she was walking towards the parking lot—I'd repeat, "Can you show me the playground or the car?" It was a process I would never take for granted.

On our way out of the park, Sierra gravitated towards the plants. She picked some flowers, pulled the petals off and apart, and sometimes the leaves. As it became more frequent, I was concerned that her nervous system was overloaded. I knew it was satiating a need, even though it seemed like a compulsion. She was attempting to find proper equilibrium in her body. I peered into those inquisitive brown eyes, letting her know I admired and loved her. Sometimes, I pulled them with her, as I placed the flower behind my ear. Then, I would offer it to her, as I asked her where she like me to place it. I would ask, "Should we put it here?" I watched her inquisitive eyes and move the flower towards where she was looking and glide alongside her. If I put it behind her ear, she might look at me, and remove it. I would say, "No", as if she were saying it to me. I would pull another with her and say, "He loves me. He loves me not…" with varied affect and tone; I gave one to her, and would watch to see if she were interested, again paying attention to any subtle cues. I would pick a few and say, "Mmmm", again. I asked her if she would like one to smell, as I looked at her and reached towards her. I would continue to pick some more. Sometimes, we made a bouquet out of them.

I was driven to give her the support she needed. To provide her with a means to an end was essential, to help her make sense and integrate further into something meaningful within our social interaction.

I aspired to stay focused on the positive, grateful for the small stuff. There was a song that we listened to, a lot. I hadn't realized the depth of meaning it held. From early on when Sierra was a baby, I'd gently toss her up in the air with excitement. I'd look into her eyes as we danced in a rhythmic fashion, upwards and downwards to a song by Train called, "Words".

"Words. They'll try to shake you. Don't let them break you or stop your world from turning. When words keep you from feeling good, use them as firewood and let them burn."

How I wished I could let them ignite into thin air and burn out all the pain. I longed to hear those WORDS, any words for that matter and those fired up, "No's!" The ones mommies often complained about as if their children were saying too much. I'd give ANYTHING to hear the sound of Sierra's VOICE. For SIERRA to enjoy life, and not to let words stop her world from turning around. "Use them as firewood, any of the words that are difficult Sierra. They will come. All of them. In your time."

Homeopathy

I continued to do more research. I called a few homeopaths. I thought that one could be a good match and I reached out to her. Also, another mom had referred her to me, whom had a child that suffered from a compromised immune system. She was nearby, about fifteen minutes away. I knew of people skyping with long distance practitioners, but I wanted her to get a clearer picture of Sierra, more personally. We started her on a combination of a few remedies. Although, I was informed that they were low in dosages. One was silicia, another was ferritin. They were 12c's Sierras prior blood test showed she was a little low in both silica and iron. She told us to use them interchangeably. They seemed to have brought out symptomologies that didn't quite fit Sierra's picture. Sierra was more hyper. She said that it could be the body's way of finding homeostasis, and that it was working effectively.

Homeopathy was odd in a way. Where did these little pellets come from? I knew it came from England or some region, but what farm? Was it organic? Homeopaths would discuss the essence and the properties contained within the remedies. When I asked where they were from, I hadn't received any more succinct answers.

Anything living was a composite of energy. The more organic, the more sufficient. Still, I tried another homeopath, as it helped some children a lot. I knew we were on this earth and had evolved for a long time and so I thought, about the composition of layering within our bodies and over time.

We decided on another homeopath. I decided to work with one that focused more classically, or at least one at a time. Since Sierra was sensitive to absorbing ingredients, I wanted to pinpoint more of what was working, more incrementally, and one at a time. Even though, it seemed like it was like finding a needle in a haystack, I was hopeful someone would pick up on her remedy picture more clearly.

The second homeopath: We traveled a little further, about a half an hour away. I found her on the web. I watched her video. She had a lot of experience along with knowledge and a passion for herbology. I was intrigued with the cathartic way she spoke about the healing qualities of plants. The homeopath had a spacious office. It was nice to be able to spread out some of my belongings. I took out some finger food for her, a couple of books, putty, and a couple of balls. I wanted to be attentive to her and respond to her questions. Sierra immediately went over to her large window sill and picked up a large gold metal ball. I saw it was difficult for her to hold and was heavy. The practitioner being intrigued by this, smiled and said, "Ohhh!" She shared something being symbolic about Sierra's gravitation to the gold ball, eluding to its spiritual components. Sierra moved about the room, picking up the ball, again from the window sill. The homeopath removed the ball from Sierra so that it didn't crash on the floor. I did my best to focus on her questions while keeping a watchful eye on Sierra. She took out a fabulous large-scale wooden train that Sierra played with for a short while. The homeopath wanted to gain insight into Sierra and my birth process. She was quite in depth in taking her notes about Sierra's physiology—Is she hot or cold at night? What does she mostly like to eat? What's her temperament like? She asked a variety of other questions as well.

The homeopath gave me a remedy that seemed to fit a person with more of a mentally erratic nature. However, I knew she had been a homeopath for a while, and I wasn't one, yet I was intuitive. Still, it was her profession. The remedy was a 200c. It seemed too high for my young toddler with sensitivities. I had asked her, how about a 30c as it's more conservative to at least start with. She said that was what fit her constitution and it had to do with energy and succession, etc. She tried to console me, and shared that she had a good feeling about it. I gave it to her a few times, once a week. Sierra was not presenting, as herself. She was acting more like the remedy, instead of her own remedy picture. I realized this was not going to work if she couldn't make a change or find value in what I was stating. I didn't understand why she couldn't be more flexible and open. We couldn't be right all of the time. Sometimes, it was essential to take a step back. A mother's intuition is called for, at times.

Oils and Other Healings

I purchased Young Living™ Oils. My basket with a plethora of oils had been growing in bounds. I had been a distributor for a few years. A great advantage was helping others who were interested in using them. I chose oils that I thought Sierra resonated the most with. I researched about how they impacted areas of the body, different organs, and the immune system, nervous systems, and others, in respect to healing. One's in particular interest of mine were for detoxing the system, for proper equilibrium in the body, and for maintaining healthy brain development. Others, I chose for ridding the body of viruses and bacteria, etc. Still others were for calming and for focus, as more secondary effects to the underlying issues, of toxic overload.

I applied the oils to the back of Sierra's neck on the base of it, on the big toe, and upon the soles of her feet. I was careful to use it sparingly, because it was concentrated. Sierra was sensitive, as well. I used a variety and rotated them. Frankincense, vetiver, lemon, thieves and any of those that contained sesquiterpenes could assist with the blood brain barrier and aid in the healing process.

I gave Sierra healings, consistently for about a year, at least four days a week. Our glider was losing its luster in terms of quality and color and hardened at the seams from overuse. However, it served a greater purpose. I rocked her and held her in my arms. I embraced all of her, as I caressed her head and gently supported her body. I asked for assistance from ascended masters, spirit guides, and her angels. I had taken classes in Integrated Angel Therapy, Pranic Healing® and utilized the merkaba, an ancient star of light and other types of healing. I applied these approaches integrating them, focusing on her chakras, sending rainbow colors of light, as I sensed areas with my hands that were more or less balanced. I would be in a more meditative state, as I allowed the energy to move through my arms, hands and fingers, and imagined spheres of light of different wavelengths in each chakra, symbolizing a different color. I started with imagining the color red on her sacral area, all the way up to violet on the crown of her head. Often, I focused on her throat with a blue healing light, and on her power center, envisioning a yellow glow. I used my hands, as a compass, to determine how strong the energy was or lacking in an area. Typically, Sierra would get so relaxed and fall asleep during this time.

I continued taking Sierra for chiropractic treatments. By receiving these adjustments, it could help balance out subluxations in the spine for greater realignment and movement of synovial fluid, for better overall health. I continued with supplements such as vitamin C, Vitamin D, B complex, minerals, etc.

I fed her mostly healthy foods. One thing she loved were lemons. She bit around the outside and work her way towards the inside. I wished eating these lemons were the answer. A bag of lemons! It contained a lot of healthful nutrients. I reminded myself that our days were sometimes pungent. We would work through it; The sweet and the sour of life.

Facing Reality

If I could allow myself to simply be, right here, right now, without feeling responsible for that which I had little control over, I could accept what was present. I reminded myself that I had the courage to change direction, to set my sights on new horizons. It was time for me to step outside of these boxes I was falling privy to, to remove the parameters that were holding me back.

On a deeper level, this was my birthright. I had an affinity for names, their meanings, and the way it metaphorically represented who we were. "Greenwald" was my maiden name, and its interpretation was green woods. Leigh my middle name signified poet. Marni, my first name, meant joyous. "The joyous poet in the green woods." I was happiest writing outside in nature, amongst the trees. I would make my way through this forest. Even in the darkest of times when the light dimmed and I felt overshadowed by those dusky clouds, the sun had a way of rising, again.

Within our rootedness, there was a more balanced state. I prayed for Sierra, for her body to align and reintegrate, for her tree to grow bountiful and beautiful with just the right amount of sunshine and water. With nurturance and with love throughout our days, my tree would stand beside her.

I was determined to weave our way through this tangled web. I had faith in mother nature, and in our own innate ability to heal. Despite the challenges we faced, both as individuals, and as mother and child, we would navigate through these paths, on our road to recovery.

I prayed throughout the days for the best possible outcome for optimal healing to occur. As I closed my eyes at night and meditated, I gained greater clarity. My heart rate slowed down, amid any racing thoughts. There was a greater calmness within, as I became more conscious of my thoughts, within controlled breaths, becoming more even. A picture I created just prior to my daughter's birth, I looked up at on her wall. A child was riding a unicorn, carried on her mother's back with a butterfly flying trailing right behind. Each night I turned to my daughter, and softly whisper, "Butterfly Kisses". I fluttered my lashes upon hers, just as she turned in. A pinkish glow formed on her cheek with a knowing stance, and a darling smile. What a beautiful butterfly you are, I'd often say.

More Education

During those days that we were in our living room play area of our cottage like home, I intermittently picked up the phone inquiring about more services, and more schooling. There was one place, a therapist and another mother had shared with me. They spoke very highly about this one program. It was located in an upscale suburban area. It was a Jewish Community Center's preschool program for children with special needs.

We made an appointment after speaking with Stella on the phone. It was a mommy and me program. How perfect to be engaged with my daughter with support, and the socialization of having other children around and being able to help guide her on her path to healing.

After our second conversation, Stella shared that this might not be the right program for our daughter, since I was a special educator and art therapist myself. She emphasized that this program was really for parents that didn't have the tools and techniques in early childhood education.

Stella expressed, "Come in anyway, if you would like, as it might be worth seeing." We went in to see the program. It wasn't close by. It was about an hour to an hour and fifteen minutes away depending on traffic. If we could go, maybe three days a week, that could be well worth our time. We walked into a beautiful newly modern structured building. The walls were primarily white with colorful pictures throughout and high ceilings.

We walked up a flight of stairs after passing security with pleasant manners, always smiling and greeting us. Up the elevator we went, and into the corridor to enter the doorway of what could possibly become my daughter's first school days. A woman approached us who was slender in stature with short, wavy, and thick silvery hair. She greeted us in a rather inquisitive and intellectual tone, with warmth.

"Hello." "My name is Stella". She shook our hands firmly. Stella turned towards Sierra, crouching down a bit, and asked "What's your name?"

"My name is Sisi". I was happily surprised, as I hadn't heard Sierra respond like that, prior.

The children were all playing in the middle of the room. The classroom was loosely structured in terms of its layout, with unstructured learning centers. The room was a nice size. I assumed the teachers were skilled enough, that their philosophy benefitted the children there. One of the teacher's looked towards us with a broad toothy smile. It was as though, she had a curiosity about Sierra, as she watched her in an inquisitive fashion. As she waved to us from across the room, she exuded a warmth about her. One mom looked over at me and smiled in a comforting way. I noticed a caring and concerned way about her. As she followed her son across the room, towards a train set, she was very attentive to him, and she engaged with him in a playful manner.

My husband, Andy and I were invited in to Stella's office. It was quaint with large windows. Sierra went over to the windowsill where there were a couple of plants. She tugged on the leaves a few times. A couple of them had fallen on the floor. Stella was a bit sharp concerning this occurrence. She said, "No" in an abrupt tone. While I understood these were her plants, and she may have been trying to teach Sierra something, it didn't sit well with me. It was just a plant, and she wasn't doing this intentionally to destroy it. I tried not to let this sway me from giving this a chance, as this was one small instance. She was human. After we had discussed some options, there was a possibility of coming three times a week to begin with. I reinforced that we had a long ride. Later on, we could possibly add on days. Stella shared it wasn't something the typically offered; however, she was willing to inquire with Human Resources about our request. It sounded as though she was interested and wanted to help us out. We left with hope in our hearts.

A New Day

I woke up to a new day. From Scratch. Yes! From scratch. Isn't that how dreams manifest. They begin with an idea. Wasn't that how the great speakers like Martin Luther King, Barack Obama, and Maya Angelo became renowned in their own right. They had a concept, one that they believed in, affirmatively. They spoke their truths with an insurmountable amount of passion and courage. Forgiveness, I told myself. Rome wasn't built in a day. Einstein, Rembrandt, Monet, and Picasso created their masterpieces within their own time.

As an artist, therapist, an educator, and outside of the box thinker, my daughter's ideas weren't going to be molded into a philosophy that weren't in alignment with hers. I thought about this clock a friend of mine designed, years ago. The word "now" was in the place of every number. What time is it again? Oh, that's right. It's now. What are we waiting for?

My daughter was intelligent, intuitive, and introspective. She was kind with an inner strength having unlimited capacities.

That song, "Words" flashed in my mind. Her fierceness would be the catalyst for her achievements, along with her innate sense of wisdom. She would navigate through obstacles, as she acclimated into her own. She would find her way through this forest, clearing any rubble. Every step she took, was progress. Even if it seemed there was a setback, it was all part of a bigger picture, not always understood.

Since Sierra was a baby, she loved looking at colors and the meanings they held. In the context of feelings found in the books she delved into she would be enamored by this. How could she not experience true emotion? She showed me her feelings in picture books from about the time she was one years old. I nudged at myself to not look back, reminding myself that there wasn't this required time line. Sierra needed to be given opportunities with respect to her challenges and her capacities, with nurturance and compassion.

Sierra was a social being. She engaged with me often, exuding these contagious belly laughs. She showed affection with hugs and kisses on my forehead. She loved to snuggle. She would take my hand and ask me to come. She looked at me ever so sweetly, into my eyes. She would grab my hand to dance, as we listened to all types of music. In many ways she was what most would refer to, as that of being a typical child.

Sierra and I enjoyed simply, being together. When I thought about the future, I envisioned her moving easily and with such grace, independently living. When doubts arose, I continued to have faith. All would happen, in due time.

Personalities
and Interests

The developmental milestones as defined in textbooks would not dictate and were not valid markers for our children's futures. I reflected on the schools of thought in our society. From a Montessori standpoint, it seemed as though very young children in order to be accepted into their program, were gifted, in such a way. I had visited a couple of Montessori schools. One concern of theirs, was that she needed an aide. While I understood their concerns, and agreed for this in some areas, they recommended hiring an ABA therapist. The director led me around the school. It was so quiet in there. I couldn't hear a pin drop. I wondered where the interaction was between children. It was all very independent work.

The Montessori approach was created by a woman named Maria Montessori to educate special needs children. My how our world had changed into a different society, placing a greater emphasis on goals. The continuum of milestones was becoming favored by the idea that children were expected to master skills at a faster rate. A world where instant gratification was met by employing principals that was on an earlier time line, beyond what young children were innately drawn to. Discovery through play, while partaking in activities that were fun and interesting. It allowed for room to grow with greater opportunities for learning at their own pace. It may not appear the same for each child, as their road took on different forms and shapes. Each one of us had our unique journeys, with paths less or more traveled. It was in these places along the way, that were to be treasured, as we developed, defined, and refined our purposes here.

The philosophy that one needs to be compliant, as in being quiet and orderly without rustling the surface by being messy, crying or having an "outburst" robs our children the honor of having a real childhood. Taking into account a child's personality and interests was necessary. To individualize concepts and avoid using cookie cutter methods to deliver the goods was essential for learning. One-dimensional work sheets had offered little support for integrating concepts for generalizing learning, alongside thematic units.

In addition, some of the aides were not trained well, not enough to truly assist children, especially those with greater needs. Some were straight out of college, while others were women returning to the work force. Many were mothers. I saw aides assisting too little or perhaps, too much. Children needed to be given the right amount of support for the aide to understand when to move forward and back, as appropriate. This took a certain understanding of child development, along with empathy, and with being intuitive enough to aid in social, emotional, and intellectual growth.

When I saw teachers or therapists hovering over or doing too much, or not giving Sierra the tools, supporting her capacity to learn while believing in her potentials, I asked myself, focus on intelligence, compassion, and having creativity. I wanted that kind of individual to be in Sierra's life. I knew I held these qualities, and would continue working with Sierra, as always. I just wished there were more teachers, who believed in her.

Was the purpose of education to obtain something for greater approval-For that gold star, so try harder, and produce more? Even when they got there and received that stamp of approval would children be happy? School was supposed to be a place where we learned tools for self-growth and achievement, well beyond the classroom. Instilling a wonder for learning with an appreciation for differences and a respect for one another, was essential. A big issue was a push for academia in preschools. Would babies be prepped to recite the Star-Spangled Banner and expected to know their alphabet at one years old? Many parents feared their child was falling behind.

The latest educational program was broadcasted on TV many times over. It was like a subliminal message that if you purchased this, your child would be the best reader, speller, or mathematician. If you didn't purchase this, "Johnny" might fall behind. Perhaps, he'd be seen as "that" kid. The one who would have the sticker on their car which said, "My kid beat up your honor roll student at _____ school…" It was quite humorous. The opposite one that I'd typically would see was, "My child is an honor roll student at _____." I'd prefer a sticker stating, "My child was the kind, student who helped _____."

In regard to special needs children, it was essential we had devoted teachers, with greater insight and compassion. Our schools needed an overhaul. For greater inclusion to build upon what we as a nation were built upon, the premise of "US", as in the United States of America; To provide our children with greater opportunities and to work together as a team. If we didn't value ourselves, as human beings with respect for all, it's a failed system. It starts in the home and into the fabric that we weave for our children. It expands within and beyond the school's walls. That way, when children enter the classroom, there is less bullying, and greater empathy.

Some teachers were parents of children who had special needs. We needed to listen attentively to each other and give what we as families could to support one another. To begin with, opening our eyes to what exists. We matter. Each of us make a profound difference in this world. Not because we are compelled to get that gold star, but because we are accepted and loved.

Let us remove the paradigm that drives our egoistic notions;
– A goal-oriented society-Striving to be the best, as in A+++
– Excessiveness of programs, emphasizing academia, beyond what was necessary, unless there was a sincere interest from the child.

Where was the process of learning, with play and social emotional intelligence including a design set up in the classroom that fosters this way of thinking? To collaborate with a partner, instilling a process-oriented approach that includes feedback from the teacher, and an optimistic attitude, motivating the students with praise, and creativity. Placing value on each of our ideas, while acknowledging different viewpoints.

Children will develop in their own time:
- By encouraging each one's abilities, to support them wherever they are at, and where there is an aha moment that he or she gets it. Capitalize on that.
- By honoring each child, slowing down, listening and interpreting the meaning within the sounds, or words, keying in on the movements during learning, and through play. By offering feedback with praise, as with proper tone and pitch, and with affect. All the "ooh's" and "aah's" with an, "Oh, I see, over here, over there." Perhaps, while pointing and showing, eliciting smiles and giggles.

Sierra would acclimate into her own body, as she explored places she gravitated to. There was no pre-set format. "Mommy and Me" continued on long after the classes ended. I held her hand. Other times, I let go. I continued to focus on the right people, places, therapists, doctors, whomever and whatever to show up-for these small miracles for Sierra.

Living in the moment is all we have. This is a certainty we can rely upon. It breeds the future. Those words from my father, "This is living" entered my mind. Dad sat in the same chair at the rounded clean, white, circular table, eating pistachio nuts with me. I watched as he carefully cracked each one, s-l-o-w-l-y, and deliberately, placing them neatly in its place. There were no words. It was time with Dad. I sat beside him, as he got messy with red dye on his hands. It wasn't about perfection. It was about the simplicity of living. He would say, "This is living" bearing a smile, and a look of gratitude.

Off to School

It was the first day of school. Sierra had been accepted into the Jewish Community Center's program held in a posh suburbia town in New Jersey. We were very excited about this new opportunity. As we walked outside our door towards the car, I took out my phone to snap a few pictures. Sierra had a light grey dress with big blue polka dots on it. There she was; my little school girl. My heart was filled with joy. I'd treasure that moment. I peered into those big brown eyes with hope that she would flourish there. A new chapter we were entering into. The trauma she experienced lingered in my mind, and I wanted to wash away any harm. With a caring and skilled staff, she would blossom. More was not always better. It was quality that mattered the most.

We had an opportunity to start fresh, on a clean slate. Besides, Sierra was young, at almost three and a half years of age. The school's emphasis was on parent-child relationships. I would be there with her, learning and growing alongside of her. This was a wonderful next step for Sierra to integrate her into a school environment. She would see that I trusted them because I was there cheering her on, being as big of support to her as I could. I was delighted to be a part of this experience, learning information, as well as, being able to assist the teachers, and parents.

We took the scenic route up the parkway where I grew up, just a few exits past it. The beautiful maple trees lined about the perimeter of the parkway we traveled on. At one point, about forty-five minutes into the trip, Sierra would start to get a bit antsy, which was completely understandable. It was about an hour drive. We would be at the program for less than three hours. It was from 9:00-11:30 am. We arrived at a large modern building. There was ample amount of parking with a good amount of people attending various programs. Upon entering, a woman at the desk greeted us. The walls had a lot of beautiful and unique art work created from children and adults. Many different classes were held there, including a music program for those with special needs. There was a lovely lounge area with a café and a juice bar. Across the way was a gift shop. Also, there was a gym that we had access to. Of course, this wasn't what we were here for, however it was nice to be able to use these services, to relax a little, from time to time.

As we walked up two flights of stairs, I could hear Sierra's feet and would observe those long strides of hers. I was happy that she was stretching and expanding those long limbs of hers, while alternating her feet. I let go of her hand, as she ran towards the large area, just steps away from the preschool room. If we got there early, sometimes we took advantage of one of the vacant rooms, while we ran around, danced and sometimes, made silly faces in the large wall to wall mirror. After we had some time there to relax into our bodies, we walked back to join the class. When we walked inside, we hung her coat up and back pack. The children would be playing with toys and scattered about the room, until it was time for morning circle. The children were called to the front of the room in a semi-circle where we sang a welcome song. Sierra was somewhat attentive, though a little fidgety at times. She tried to acclimate herself, as best she could. On some days she was more relaxed, and sat for longer periods.

The class was divided into two groups for reading. A more advanced one and the other, for those needing more support. One child had a genius-like intelligence. His mom shared he had albinism and was nearly blind. He was a couple of years older. She continued that he had some attention issues, and undesirable behaviors. There was also a little girl diagnosed with selective mutism, and another, a girl with physical challenges who spoke two languages. There was another boy, who was tongue tied at birth with some attention issues. Lastly, there was one other little boy, named Aidan. He was unique, distinct from Sierra, but there was definitely something similar about them. I learned from meeting his mom, Jennifer, that he suffered from auto-immune issues. Sierra did too, yet I hadn't known the specifics of it. We became fast friends. She was warm, compassionate and understanding. At the group support meetings held once a week, moms would come together and discuss their concerns on different topics. Ours seemed different, for reasons of our children's challenges being much more complex.

Sierra was not flourishing there. Although the program was play based, there was a lot of focus on compliance, then I had originally thought. I was hoping for the teachers and therapists to feel comfortable with following her lead more, giving her the space within opportunities to acclimate. As Sierra was able to relax, and regulate more, the information could be received with greater ease as she could engage in an activity she enjoyed for longer periods of time.

Often, the staff acknowledged behaviors by drawing happy and sad faces with black marker on white paper. They said, "It's okay to be happy" as they drew a smiley face. This was followed by, "It's okay to be sad, as they drew a sad face. Somewhat simple, I surmised. You are allowed to be sad and allowed to be happy. It appeared as though they wanted children to be able to maintain a happy outlook, after they were deregulated or emotionally unable to contain a more acceptable state of being. Talking about one's feelings was essential, and not extinguishing them when we felt it was necessary. Listening to a child's thoughts and feelings was key. There was such meaning in the process. A more beneficial and respectful goal would not be to wipe away emotions, but to acknowledge them and find out the underlying reasons in a compassionate way.

Both the occupational and speech therapist that she was assigned to, seemed as though they didn't understand Sierra's needs well. Entering her world through play was essential. Realizing that sometimes she just needed for them to just be, and slow down, to relax without a set goal in mind. She had severe apraxia, proprioceptive, and vestibular issues. Like any child, she needed to feel heard. What she didn't have, like many children had were more apparent and congruent fluid coping mechanisms. To fold one's hands and participate by listening to the teacher, even if they didn't enjoy it—How effective was learning?

I found out that the speech therapist was using these bubble gum flavored latex gloves, as I came into her office one day. I heard Sierra crying and nearing the end, I gave a little knock on the door. When we started the program, I informed Stella and the speech therapist, to kindly refrain from using any latex, as she had a sensitivity to this. It contained chemicals and synthetic fillers. It could contain gluten, or other toxic substances in the flavoring.

The room was extremely small and filled to the rim with books and toys. The speech therapist was a voluptuous and rather boisterous woman whose presence could be intimidating, in tiny quarters. I shared with the director, Stella, early on that I had concerns. I asked about the other speech therapist, even though she had less training and fewer years of working in this field. She believed the more seasoned speech therapist was more appropriate for Sierra's needs.

The philosophy of this parent child program had become less apparent to me. It was advertised as a program where parents were welcomed. Yet, there were many restrictions. From the very beginning, I was not permitted to go into the speech room. None of the parents were. I didn't understand this and was concerned about the minimal opportunities given to me and the rest of the parents who attended there. Sierra had global apraxia, hyptonia, and sensory integration disorder. It would prove to be beneficial to be part of both the speech therapy and occupational therapy sessions for continued learning and growth.

The occupational therapist confided to me that she didn't understand where the "behaviors" such as more excessive crying were coming from. One day, I walked into the O.T. room to find Sierra laying on a bean bag with Stella, the O.T., and the social worker standing over her. An opened bag of gluten free pretzels I noticed just above the mats, nearby. Apparently, they were using this to console her. Somewhat startled, I asked them what they were doing with the bag of pretzels. Stella shared that they thought they would try using them. I asked in a concerned, yet disappointed tone, "Did they help?" Stella chuckled, and in a somewhat embarrassed way replied, "Actually, no…". She knew I wasn't in favor of using food and admitted that this wasn't going to work.

On another occasion, the occupational therapist confided to me, "I think Sierra might have this rare disorder." I was rather stunned. The name she referred to had escaped me. I felt like we were on some other planet, as we were not being acknowledged and understood.

Out

After about five months, we realized that we were nearing the end of our journey at the preschool. It was never on my radar that there would be such ignorance and discrimination against a child. I guess she had greater challenges than what they deemed appropriate. As disheartening as it was, I knew it was time to move on. The profile of their program didn't fit what I saw as helping children with special needs. It appeared as though acceptance into their program included a narrower spectrum, such as selective mutism or children with a mild attention issue. I thought people in this profession would want to help those children's struggling more. It seemed if children were already speaking, sitting more functionally, following directions with more integrated motor planning, etc., were a better fit for them. I heard the program was not thriving, as well as it had. When districts would observe or individual parents observed, if I child had less issues to begin with, it could represent them as a program where children made more obvious gains.

What baffled me the most, was when I conversed with another parent to discover something, quite unethical. Her little girl had recently started the program. It was brought to my attention that she was waiting for scholarship funds to be coming, soon. I couldn't help, but deduce that this was most likely, our scholarship money, now that we were leaving the program. All those smiley and sad faces faded right before my eyes.

An Enticing Opportunity

We embarked on continuing to observe other preschools for Sierra. One promising place was the Marcus Center, located at a well-known university. It was an inclusion program that offered a child centered approach with the floortime methodology, as a large component. We decided to open up Sierra's file and had contacted our case manager at our local school district. Sierra needed to be evaluated by the occupational therapist and speech therapist at her current placement. The team agreed to send her file to this center, as well.

One bright spring afternoon, Sierra and I drove from her current preschool to the Marcus Center, to interview with them. I was nervous, yet excited for this promising opportunity. Something that sounded as though it could meet her needs, more appropriately. Sierra brought in one of her favorite books, "Goodnight Moon". We both were invited into the O.T. room after meeting with our case manager and director in the doorway. Sierra moved towards the large play structure. She climbed up the ladder, as the O.T. was several feet away from her. She acted playfully, with attentiveness towards Sierra's movements and her expressions. She positioned her body towards her and in an animated way exclaimed, "Hi, over there". She paused and waited, observing what Sierra would partake in next.

Sierra climbed towards the top, as she clutched her book at hand. Just as she went down the slide, she dropped the book upon the floor. She laughed giddily, while she moved in a circular fashion. The room appeared to be designed in such an ergonomic fashion, and it was bright and airy. Sierra went over to the sand table that had figurines. The O.T. watched Sierra's movements, as she interjected herself by holding up a figure and moving it slowly, while simultaneously connecting with her. She exhibited a lot of intonation in her voice, and a very warm and friendly presence about her.

More teachers and therapists had entered the room and introduced themselves. It was the director of the program, a speech therapist, and physical therapist. The early childhood specialist came over and asked me what Sierra's interests were. After the director, led Sierra and I into the teacher's classroom. She introduced us to the teacher. All the children were gathered in a circle, as the teacher read a story to them. She glanced up and gave a smile. I waved back. The room had lots of toys in an organized fashion and with learning centers. It was a very multi-sensory hands on based program. We were told there were eighteen children in the class, and that three with learning challenges had been accepted into the program. They had space for one more child with special needs, as they allotted four in each class.

I shared with one of the educator's that Sierra had to use the bathroom. As we were brought inside, Sierra motioned to me that she had to use the potty. I was elated, and relieved to see her this comfortable. The bathroom was set up with child sized toilets. It was designed to meet the needs of the children. Soon after, I saw from across the room, our case manager exchanging words with the staff, and inquiring about what seemed to be a concern for distractibility, due to class size and noise levels. I continued to listen in with one ear, while playing with Sierra in the back of the classroom in the sand box area. Their team appeared to be amenable to having Sierra there, as I noticed them nodding supportively, answering the case manager's questions, in what seemed to be a more positive intent.

Overall, it was a great experience. The staff worked in tandem with each other and addressed children's needs from a more social emotional perspective. The observation went well. Just as we walked outside the bright building, I let out a sigh of relief. Perhaps, we found a place with an approach that worked best for Sierra. My case manager called over to me just as we left and were outside the building. She asked if we were happy with the program. With controlled enthusiasm, I nodded a favorable, "Yes".

As we walked back to our car and I opened the door, I saw that spark in Sierra's eyes, one that I hadn't seen in a while. Perhaps, a sense of belonging, a more accepting place. It was a bit far from home, but a wonderful program. We were called to sign a contract by our case manager. We were informed that Sierra was accepted into the program. On July 11, 2014, my birthday, I went in to sign the agreement at our school's administrative offices. One area I was concerned about on the IEP (Individualized Educational Program) was that it stated that all of the therapies were group supported, not individualized sessions. This concerned me because

I was always told what Sierra needed was, "Individual, individual, individual." Still, I left with a good feeling about opportunity. Little did I know how rare it was.

Our New Home

O ur neighborhood was a little more suburban then our prior
town. It had a lovely town center. Surely, Sierra would get
an optimal education here. I had researched and read about the
schools with the highest ratings in this county. This was one of
them listed. I inquired about the Director of Special Education,
whom I was told was gave the children what they needed. I spoke
with the Head of Child Study Teams in order to gain as much
valuable information as I could. He became a useful resource,
a knowledgeable and compassionate person. I called upon him
when I had questions, so that our daughter could be taught
appropriately, and get the services she needed.

We sold our house to a lovely couple. Shortly after we accepted
their offer, and they put the down payment down and were approved
by the bank, I began to have doubts. I loved our quaint cottage
home. My husband expressed to me that there was no turning back.
We made our decision. It was finalized. Our house was sold.

It was the month of August. That meant moving time. Sierra
and I decided to stay at my parent's house over the course of two

weeks. Andy was kind enough to get the house ready for all of us. That last day before we returned home, I received a phone call from the Director of the Marcus Center. She inquired about when we would come in and meet with the new teacher. I was reluctant; as we were moving to a new town and wanted to be sure we made the best decision for Sierra. I pondered, "Was it better to be part of a community in walking distance from our home or would we would be better served at the Marcus Program?" I would meet with the child study team before making a decision.

Although my heart had been set on the program at the Marcus Center, the program in our district was worth trying. As Andy, Sierra, and I made our way into the Board's office of administration meeting room, we saw many new faces, at least ten that were present at this rather long table. They introduced themselves, accordingly, all having various positions as employees within the district. They asked us questions about Sierra and her developmental needs. They reviewed her past experiences and evaluations. They informed us about their preschool program. The case manager concluded that their program would meet the needs for our daughter. It was a special class for learning disabilities that served up to twelve children. There were four classes in total. The assistant of special education showed compassion. A big concern of ours was that she was not, yet consistently using the bathroom. Her response to this, was in a sweet and patient tone, "That's okay, she's not ready yet." I ascertained, perhaps we were in the right place. As I watched Sierra move swiftly about the large sterile white room, in the back of my mind, I thought, Sierra deserves a chance to be a part of this community and make friends. It seemed like the children there would be good peer models for her. Besides,

I had visited the classrooms prior to this meeting. I gathered it was a supportive and integrated program. The children seemed happy and the staff seemed dedicated and caring. At the end of the hallway was a different program. I was informed by the director of this program that it wasn't an ABA philosophy. She stated that it was whatever the children needed, with a multi-sensory approach. I looked the program up on the web. It emphasized this.

We took home the Individualized Educational Program to review it, before signing it. I went back and forth about it. I reminded myself, nothing was permanent. We moved here to be part of a community. I decided to sign it. I hadn't realized it was one of the biggest decisions that would impact Sierra's, and our family's lives.

Our Backyard

Our backyard was quaint with lovely trees, fairly private. This excited us most in making the decision to move here, and what would become our new home. It was about a half an acre, with a lowland hill running down from the top of it. Perfect for Sierra to play outside on and served as a perfect size for her wooden play set with a swing, a slide and small abode up on top to be set up upon. Also, we were looking forward to giving her the safest and sturdiest trampoline which she received on her fifth birthday. Surely, she would revel in jumping on it, springing high up in the air, and outside amongst the trees in nature. Sierra loved the outdoors, hiking, picking flowers etc. Our daily outing to the farm was always a joy for us as she ate herbs such as basil, and garlic chives, and raw vegetables, such as dinosaur kale and sorrel lettuce. Here, we could grow them. It would be a wonderful place to garden.

Our Street

Our street was a mixture of young and old, with some young children residing here. Just next door, there was a little girl, a couple of years older than Sierra. Frequently, Clara emerged from her backyard. Briskly, she walked over beyond the open area of streamlined trees. She smiled and waved hello. We let her know that she was always welcome here. She hopped on over, gayly, in a friendly way. She ran towards the trampoline my husband and Sierra were jumping on. Sometimes, I jumped on it as well. Her mom came over briefly from time to time, for several months, though the family wasn't in the backyard much. I'd seldom see them unless they took their dogs out.

We often played music. Clara loved Taylor Swift. Sierra seemed as though she admired Clara and enjoyed her company. Sierra reached over to hug Clara. She was sometimes reluctant. I'd let her know that Sierra was just showing her affection and really liked her. Sierra was communicating with her, infrequently, stroking her arms, wanting to engage with her. She happily jumped with Clara on the trampoline. We offered to give them snacks. I'd call Clara's mom and ask if it was okay, which it was, typically. During her time here, she said she had to find out from her parents if she could stay a little longer. She returned, almost always saying excitedly, "Ten more minutes".

As the months went by, Clara made her appearance here less. She disappeared from not only our backyard, but our lives. When we did see her outside, she wasn't as friendly towards us, and often turned her head. Sierra would wait in the backyard for her, as she stood adjacent to the trees. You could see the windows of her house from here. It was as though, there was this dividing line. I didn't understand what happened. I saw glimpses of Clara from time to time with soccer gear on, or dance outfits. I suppose she moved on from partaking in any fun with us.

We became friendly with the dog walkers. No one judged Maggie. She was a dog. She was sprite, pretty, and predictable. In the early morning, after Sierra got picked up from transportation for school, I saw our dog walking friends. Typically, Andy walked Maggie on the weekends. Maggie would sit on her favorite chocolate couch by the window in front of our living room. She howled or barked in the early mornings. Andy grabbed the leash and say, "C'mon Maggie. Let's go." Some down time to socialize with the neighbors.

Not many, if anyone, understood our world. Still, there was good ol' Arthur. He was a retired man who lived down the street. He offered to help out in any way he could. He was a kind endearing man, whom we had referred to as the mayor of our street. He looked out for people, simply because he cared.

Reflections

In my twenty plus and early thirty something years, life was much different. The balance within each sphere of influence was more easily distributed in terms of career, health and in nurturing my closest relationships with family and friends.

These days, I was caught in a space that was unchartered territory. That pie that was given to us in those psychology classes. It showed the areas essential within our lives, to be bracketed off with a percentile into what we had in terms of equilibrium to acknowledge and observe whether our needs were being met. In addition, I wondered how we would balance those areas such as in family, career, relationships, etc. My life was not even close to being evenly distributed. This one area was so pronounced and was growing larger in scope.

This one image had eluded my mind. I sat at the bottom of an inverted sand castle. More like a ditch, my knees pressed firmly into my chest with my left hand in the sands, my right hand holding a lantern. This vision had become all too familiar. As the days passed, so did this jar-like existence, like an hourglass being filled up, it turned over and over, again—from daylight until dusk. It was like Groundhogs Day.

It was morning, again. As I rolled over in my bed, I emerged into this external world, one that wasn't very forgiving. I dragged myself out from under the covers and stretched my limbs. As if I were a tree bending to one side and then the other, I rolled my shoulders forwards and then back, again. I felt slightly more limber and more open. The large mirror, I glanced up at. Hurriedly, I grabbed some yogi clothing from my wooden drawer. I had been attending classes three or four days a week. It was my saving grace. As I tucked my head into a tightly woven sports bra, throwing on a more comfortable shirt over it, I looked at my petite, pear shaped body. I was one of those women with fuller hips. It was okay. I was a woman, after all. During yoga class as I looked at their large mirror encompassing the entire wall, those hips would remain the most prominent part of me. While I knew this was unimportant, sometimes, those imperfections, came to surface. It was kind of a distraction from the bigger things. Yoga helped me, immensely. I stretched my "inner" in the practice of yoga, as I released any tensions, and blocks standing in my way.

As I turned the corner to go downstairs, I was conscious of the two stairs that creaked in the mornings. I hadn't wanted to wake Sierra up. I entered our white, nineteen sixties outdated kitchen, and prepared my wake me up cup o' coffee. I would glide through the dining room and towards the bathroom. As I washed my face, I began noticing those fine lines becoming more apparent. The hardships and the beauty were becoming more recognizable to me. I reminded myself that each one of these lines were telling a story. A story with lots of character.

Lost Time

More than ever, I needed to make up for "lost" time. I stalked myself in the car. I became my own therapist. Engaging in back and forth conversation during both shorter drives and those of longer duration—This was throughout the course of the day, in between all I encountered on a daily basis and any chatter going on inside of me. This "talking" would help me through any pain or understanding surfacing or resurfacing. Along with the music that accompanied me on my rides, messages I would hear from lyrics soothed me and helped me get deeper in touch with something pivotal. I continuously released what didn't serve me. In those subtle moments, I'd get that aha moment, as if I had an epiphany.

If I was cut off by a driver or tail gaited, I would get into this fierce mode. Though, I didn't want anger to get the best of me. That feisty, tenacious part of me would emerge with courage. That "solvent to the solution" I was willing to discover, in whatever way, whatever form it took. I would take a breather, as I reminded myself to remain in the moment, when pangs of doubt resurfaced.

At forty-seven years of age, I hoped I was growing wiser. Yet, what had been presented to me was not wrapped up in a pretty pink box with a white bow. I realized that in the garden we tend to sometimes—yes, sometimes life gives us lemons. And it wasn't as simple as squeezing out the juice or making lemonade with it. The lemons fell wherever they may. Each one ripened in and of their own time.

At times, I felt more empowered. I affirmed, "I can handle this!" That existentialism philosophy I gravitated to years back was inherent within me that "whatever is, ye shall become."

As I acknowledged the greater "I" of who I was, I looked further within, unraveling stored emotions that crept up on me from time to time. These needed to be peeled away. That old worn out notion of being two years behind lurked somewhere in the shadows. When the tears came, it provided somewhat of a release. I was ready to begin again.

I realigned myself with the seers; The gifted and compassionate souls, the ones that could empathize with something not always obvious, or easily seen on the surface. Sierra and I were not meant to be "giver uppers". She was one of the most strong-willed people I had ever known. I encouraged her, as I asked her lots of questions about the who's, and what's, and where's, and sometimes the why's and how's of people, places, and things. Also, I posed questions as, "I wonder what would happen if?" Just as I did, as a child. We did this thing called life, together.

Preschool Program

It was the first day of school. Our cars lined the perimeter of the curbside or we could park in the lot that spanned it. Ms. Radner, Sierra's teacher came over, shook my hand and smiled. She leaned over to Sierra with a warm welcome. I saw some children line up beside the aide, and one by one, noticing that they were all boys. One little boy stood out. I later found out his name was Jayme's. He seemed to take an immediate liking to Sierra. He had a bright toothy smile with big blue eyes. Ever since that very first day, he gravitated over to her. He trailed behind her and took her hand, even when Sierra turned away shyly or appeared uninterested. He was really such a love. He had a real love of the color pink. Pink cars, Peppa Pig and pink nail polish. Having him in Sierra's life was truly a blessing.

Jaymes's mom and I took a liking towards each other and became fast friends. We had similar philosophies. When the going got tough and placement didn't seem right for Sierra, she shared that she went to the Marcus program in which the floor time was a better fit for Sierra. Jaymes had gone to the school when he was a toddler.

All the children in Sierra's class were speaking, and quite fluidly. Sierra struggled with this, and with coordinating body movements. Little did we know what difficulty it would be to move her out of here. We were eager for her to attend the Marcus Center program where she had originally been accepted by the former district. We had several letters from skilled doctors and therapists sharing that Sierra needed more of a movement based, social emotional program encouraging language. Neurologists and developmental pediatricians, our former speech therapist, and our supervisor from Aspen Trails, who was from an ABA program, shared this with us. My husband and I met with the team to discuss options.

Dr. Sambuca, the new Director of Special Education, was set against this program. The team shared their program was more suited for Sierra's needs. We were told the former one was more amicable in working with the parents. I saw that I was in for something, way over my head. However, my passion turned into a fierceness, when it pertained to our daughter.

The process seemed incredibly long and a tedious one, at that. We had hired a special education advocate. She was knowledgeable and had expertise in a variety of areas. However, she didn't speak up much. I spoke up a lot during the meeting. I suppose it was my voice to be heard. Michelle Farida presented my case to the Supervisor, Ms. Sambuca. She concluded that the appropriate place was for Sierra to remain at the preschool she was, currently at.

Heart

During those days at the preschool program we could have experienced something greater, as in representing the more gratifying aspects of a world leading with kindness. The methodology adhered more to standards of early childhood academia and catching up to these principals. All these tabulated goals had to be met for state requirements. The children's IEP's had to be filled out, accordingly. What would come easiest in terms of actual work, would take precedence over loving their jobs. I don't know, I suppose people were busy; therapists had large caseloads and juggling different schools. As parents, it was up to us to fill in "the gaps". The over utilized approach of ABA was being adopted in most places. Children were not incompetent, nor to be undermined. Children were more capable than the simplicity and domination of this type of philosophy. There was nothing wrong with cognitive approaches in helping with behavior, but not at the forefront and not without taking consideration the individual's social abilities and apraxia challenges. I hadn't understood if others weren't interested in being more creative or was it that they lacked a greater understanding allowing for more intimacy in letting down their guards, thus allowing for a more social relationship to be formed. If a child didn't achieve these goals set by the teachers and therapists, they were stuck on these set of skills before new one's could be taught. What about trying a different approach, to consider teaching it for a different response. Where was the wiggle room allowing for greater responsiveness to skills by changing one's method to meet the needs of the child, instead of expecting a child to do a set of tasks according to the same approach.

It appeared as though, Sierra's aids took direction from the teacher with little attention to their own abilities to assist children. I was invited in to observe a speech session. Sierra went over to the book shelves which surrounded a good portion of one wall in a small space. She felt comforted by utilizing them. The aide stood up with her arms outstretched, as she blocked off access to the books. She pointed to the chair and said, "Sit down" in a monotone voice, bearing little affect. Then, the speech therapist minimized her usage of words with directives such as, "Put in box." "Take out box." This was an ineffective strategy for building reciprocity and expanding upon a natural engagement of play with trust. This was limiting for Sierra's range of understanding as well, in terms of her scope of knowledge. Why would anyone want to share their thoughts from this type of interaction? A greater insight into human behavior by having empathic responses would prove to be more valuable in terms of communication.

"Sierra-Pick a letter." "Put in box." I observed the therapist prompting Sierra to do this several times. She read the book "Five Little Ducks", as she wrote in the log book, as I observed her a couple of times. While I understood it was a song and that it was rhyming, sometimes too much of something, anything, could prove to be ineffective. The therapy room that was small and square room was appearing like a metaphor to me. Sierra was not a Jack in the box, or in this case, "a Sierra in the box".

Boxes Shmoxes

The way I felt about boxes was that they served a purpose, not only for holding goods. When they were emptied, we needed to be creative with them. You know—pour beans, sand, or buttons into them. Build with them, both the small and large ones. Step inside the larger ones. Use them as pretend play. Make a boat. Get in and row it. Grab some sticks for oars. Be the child within you.

All the I-Pads and technology with these programs were provided on a three-dimensional format, on smart boards, etc. We needed to use our own imagination stations along with our brains and our bodies to not be held hostage to a screen for learning. In addition, these days, children were accustomed to going from the womb learning about the ABC's and Dr. Seuss, to early reader books and the like. "What about Play? "What About Us?" Like Pink's song children were not to be forgotten. They need to be tended to as the capable, intelligent, beautiful soul's they are. It was essential for them not to be taught within only a heady structure, based upon a super goal-oriented society to get to where? Over there? It was too soon, and too fast. This type of teaching negated our capacity to utilize our truest gifts. If we allowed our children to find where "over there" was by using their imaginations, they could develop more naturally, wherever "there" was. Not to have a preconceived notion of what the lesson actually was, but to prepare for anything to happen, with guidance from taking the child's lead and interests into consideration. An extinguish reward, response system was not favorable in valuing the interaction between two people. This was where real learning occurred. It was fun and it was enticing. It was as simple, as that.

Preschool

Ms. Radner was a skilled teacher with years of experience, kind of traditional, and very hands on. She'd make things out of various sized boxes, egg crates, and paper towel rolls. One day as I walked into school to pick Sierra up, as I usually had, I noticed the wonderful creation she was constructing. She had been working with the children on making a car wash. She used different sized boxes, larger ones for the cars, paper towel rolls, and jars for the wheels, rubber bands securing them, tempera paints, large scarves as one entered the car wash, and other areas.

Typically, I picked Sierra up at 11:45 as I knew due to Sierra's immune challenges, she would tire. Behaviors were oft looked at something to be extinguished and rewarded. Sierra needed the simplicity of being understood, as in acknowledging her to cry, as a healthy form of communication. These behaviors needed to be understood as such and utilized to support Sierra while reinforcing receptive and expressive areas. With empathy and with patience stemming from one's intuitive understanding of interpreting another's emotions.

There I was. Same bat channel, same bat time. I came knocking on the door at 11:45 before lunch. Ms. Radner opened the door with a soft voice and simple greeting. She was somewhat warm, yet I sensed an apprehensiveness about her, regarding Sierra's needs. From her quick and short responses, it appeared as though, she believed Sierra needed more.

Sierra was returning to class from the speech therapist's room, just down the hall. As she proceeded to walk, the therapist spoke, "Walk down", "Room A". She pointed with an outstretched arm, almost as they entered the door to the classroom—"Open door." Her words struck me as having an oversimplified and stern tone. I smiled at Sierra with a reassuring look and said hello. Then, she was directed in, as if she were a robot. My heart sank in disbelief.

Ms. Radner intentionally dropped Sierra's jacket on the floor. I had seen her participate in this type of strategy prior. Sierra picked it up. Next, was the prompt, "Put on." Ugh! I thought. Why wasn't she treated with more respect? She was a human being, besides being capable and intelligent. This was undermining her potential. Using a natural approach in regularity of speech in a flow of words, was much more appropriate for her, especially since she had global apraxia. The speech therapist and supervisor shared that they didn't think Sierra had apraxia because they didn't hear her producing enough words. They said it was more pragmatic that she needed first and foremost. Restricting oneself from performing, as in limiting the parameter of words into these non-generalized offerings was ineffective for Sierra's needs. Sierra had an expressive language challenge; however, receptively and emotionally she understood. This would only cause a further distrust and unwillingness to comply to what the teachers were expecting. To adjust to a standard with an approach that was rigid and demanding, was not going to work.

I called Ms. Farida, the Assistant to the Special Education Supervisor the day this happened. She shared that they were utilizing a Montessori technique. Yet, it was like Sierra was being hovered over by the therapist in the room, and her teacher who deliberately, dropped it on the floor. Both of their tones of voice could have been much more amicable.

In-Visible

We fought tooth and nail to find a more appropriate placement for Sierra. In these team meetings, I felt as though
my voice was echoing in the background more often than not. If
it was heard, it was not welcomed, and mostly responded to with
silence. If anything was communicated, which was far and few
between questions I asked, it was ignoring my request or derailing
my statements about pertinent issues. I was articulate, did my
research, and was tirelessly passionate.

Sierra was tested verbally, and because of this her scores were
low. This was not a valid test of her intellect. She had a severe
expressive language challenge. We weren't informed about an
option for non-verbal testing, and they gave her all verbal tests. In
their conclusion of her cognitive strengths, it was invalid, due to
her apraxia. They wouldn't give her credit in any unresponsiveness
to answering questions. There wasn't a program for communication challenges, especially in ideomotor apraxia. Therefore, one
could justify keeping her in a program within their school that may
not be best suited for her, and with a style of teaching methodology

that may not be beneficial for her needs. They had to modify it. The speech therapists shared that Sierra didn't have apraxia, however we had letters from her long-standing speech therapist that she had a fairly significant apraxia component. Other means of expressing, such as signing from a very young age never came easy for Sierra, as she had ideomotor apraxia, so the messages within her body took a longer time to access. Sierra needed a least restrictive environment with children who were expressing more verbally from a social standpoint, and with a methodology that focused on building language taking into consideration movement and regulation within the body. Sierra was given an opportunity to be placed in an environment with children with multiple disabilities. It was a fairly new program that had been implemented a year ago, within the district.

I was reluctant. I had Sierra retested with an outside psychologist who shared her I.Q. was twenty-two plus points higher than the schools more verbal type of testing revealed. She shared she wanted to give her credit for several answers, however her pointing was not exactly, uniform, or she was a bit distracted. We decided to place Sierra in their program, as we weren't presented with any other viable option. I remembered a case manager shared early on at one of our team meetings, when Sierra was in the preschool program, that the following year, they had some fabulous programs. She commented that the teachers were wonderful and how much we'd be happy with it. I was interested in the learning-disabled program, however members of the team shared that it was not appropriate, as her needs were greater.

The Class

Her class included six children. There was a variety of differing abilities in the small class. Half the children had a diagnosis of down syndrome. One other, a nine-year old girl, four years older than my little kindergartener we were told had behavioral challenges, and a boy who had intellectual challenges. I was about inclusion for all abilities. It was essential for Sierra to have role models that would support her speech and communication, and overall development. With respect to her as an individual, more peer modeling while being in an inclusive type of setting for at least some of the day would prove to be more helpful for her needs. Plus, Sierra was the only kindergartener. The rest were at least two years older. Having the opportunity to be friends with a little girl, whom Sierra could form a relationship with could make a big difference in her life.

We started Sierra in the program in the summertime. It was held at the Wiscott School, a different school in the district for the summer. Sierra's new teacher was young, with a bubbly kind of disposition. She appeared optimistic and genuinely interested in helping Sierra. After several weeks, I was growing concerned at some of the work that was being presented to Sierra. One was of a time line created on a strip of manila paper and black pen with the numbers one through ten. Sierra had to label the numbers when asked. Sierra knew her numbers at least up to thirty to correctly identify them and probably, more so. However, it may have been inconsistent due to fine motor, or an attention issue caused by a vestibular, or proprioceptive challenge. The next best thing was to share with her, in hopes that she listened in learning more about Sierra, and what she was capable of. I knew that this was the summertime and methodologies were taught on the lighter side. As she got to know Sierra, she'd challenge her more.

Sierra was soon to be on a long road trip with her dad and me. We had spent months conversing with Cord Blood Registry and corresponding with Duke University. We sent a variety of documents including blood tests, and doctor's reports of Sierra's diagnoses. A most prominent one, being global apraxia. She was accepted to be a part of a compassionate independent study. She would receive her own umbilical cord stem cells. It kept me going in these stressful times. I picked Sierra up from her days at her school's program. I watched her walk with great strides with her back pack on. She walked boldly, with a skip in her step. She was articulating a little more. It gave me greater hope.

Stem Cells

We packed up our grey Prius, and we set out on our eight-hour trip to Duke University. I purchased Sierra some more art supplies, and a great little art case. It was purple which was one of her favorite colors, as well as, yellow. Sierra's name was painted on it. She could prop it up towards the front seat for support and watercolor and draw with different mediums. Inside there was space for her favorite dress up doll sticker books, etc.

We stopped at rest places, mostly to utilize the bathroom. Andy was always helping out. I had called him Mighty Mouse, as he was always there to offer support, to save the day, and performed kind deeds for others. Typically, Andy brought Sierra to the family room, if it was available. He took pleasure in being there for Sierra, and he wanted to give me some time for myself. These little things meant a lot to me. We worked well, together as a team.

I prayed that stem cells would alleviate some of these challenges. There was a lot of information about how musculoskeletal and neurological conditions were being treated. Children and adults were being healed. However, insurance didn't cover stem cells in the US. We would be the pioneers of something on the horizon, an intervention that could work.

We got to our hotel in Durham, North Carolina. It was a smooth sailing ride. Sierra was the greatest little traveler. She loved the car. She always had since she was a baby. She was an independent one. During that car ride, I reflected back to her days at the Little Gym, where for two years she went from aged two to four years old. Her young dance teacher, who taught gymnastics there, told us that Sierra's made the most progress she had ever seen of all the children there. Those words remained with both my husband and me. It brought such joy my heart. Sierra was a determined little girl, and if given a chance, was not only going to compensate for her challenges, yet heal.

After dropping off our belongings in the mediocre hotel, with two twin beds in one small room, and a tiny living room area, though hospitable, we ventured out in Durham, North Carolina's territories. We were thrilled to be able to find a Whole Foods Market, as that was our go to place for healthier foods. All of us would be able to find something nourishing and delicious there. Maybe, we liked it too much, as we spent much of our time there. We found some of Sierra's favorite things to eat, salmon sushi with avocado and roasted chicken. Sierra also enjoyed some salad greens and ate some vegetables, though minimally. She ate kale and other green herbs raw. Sierra had a rather large appetite for a little person. She could eat close to a whole chicken in one sitting.

After we munched out at Whole Foods Market, we took a turn to the hospital for a routine check-up. The nurse was present and inquired about Sierra's background asking questions about Sierra's history, medical, intellectual, on development, and psychological questions. Typical information gathered for the hospital for insurance purposes and gathered to support other children with similar issues in studies being done. We were interested in understanding more about how the stem cells would impact Sierra, after receiving them. We were in the initial stages in gathering information about children, and so not much was documented in texts, yet about stem cells and neurological conditions. The nurse checked her height and weight. It was in "normal range" for a child of her age, at five years old. After about an hour or so, we left, and were to return the next day for the cells. She shared that the treatment would be about fifteen minutes. It consisted of having an IV in her arm where the cells would be delivered. Prior to that, they'd give her a mild steroid. They agreed to refrain from giving her any Tylenol or aspirin.

The next morning arrived. We were punctual, as we couldn't wait! We took the elevator up to the floor that was primarily for bone marrow transplant infusions. A little girl was present with her mother. They were friendly and open to sharing. The mother spoke kindly, having a broad smile. Willingly, she informed us that her daughter received donor cells from her sister for cancer treatment. They had transfusions to hopefully give their child a greater quality of life. I told her how wonderful that was, truly a gift. To have a daughter whose sister could donate to her, how kind of her to support her sister. We made a nice connection with another family going through a traumatic experience. It touched me deeply, reminding me of the unique bond we shared, connecting us, as human beings. We have frailties, and we have strengths. Families supporting each other, sharing one another's experiences, was indeed beautiful.

The duration of time we waited for the frozen cells to arrive was longer than we anticipated. We went downstairs to keep Sierra occupied and walked around a bit. The front desk had a basketball, so the three of us played at the court just outside in front of the hospital. Some fun for Sierra was helpful, especially in the heat of this exciting but nerve provoking experience. Shortly after, we returned upstairs where Sierra had some guacamole and pretzels. Then, we were brought into a small private room. Our very caring and dedicated nurse we had formed a relationship with, was present with us. We had many phone conversations with her and were thankful she had guided us through this long, arduous process. She was such a great support to us, and willingly offered as much help as she could to get us there with the most comfort and least amount of stress.

When the music therapist came in, he asked if there were any songs that Sierra enjoyed. We shared about her love for Bob Marley —"One Love" and "Don't Worry about a Thing", and Sesame street songs, etc. He played his guitar and sang, as Sierra was being prepped and given a local steroid. She had the IV attached to her arm then. The doctor came in and introduced herself as Dr. Sun. Let the sunshine in. What better sunshine brought to us, as Sierra's own stem cells being given to her. Dr. Sun called a blood technician in to assist in getting the butterfly of the IV into Sierra's arm, upon having some difficulty. Sierra was a trooper. We were so proud of her. Andy's eyes welled up, as I could sense his gratitude. We gave each other a warm embrace.

I was so thankful to the music man who held that fine guitar and sang some of Sierra's favorite songs during a large part of this.

I held Sierra's hand, as I laid beside her. As I peered into those big brown eyes of hers, I knew all would be okay.

Shortly after, Sierra fell asleep when she had been given water through an IV. She rested for about an hour. It was time to allow those cells to disperse where they needed to go most; hopefully, for healing to occur. Sierra woke up a little groggy, though that was to be expected. Soon after, she got up and out of bed with a smile, ready and raring to go.

Focusing on Sierra's Strengths

Sierra needed to be challenged by the teacher, the speech therapist, and O.T. It was essential to capitalize on Sierra's strengths and all that she was capable of learning. In addition, our home school had been reluctant in providing her with an assistive device, an IPAD. It had been over two years since I first requested it. It was considered unnecessary. It was to support her as an adjunct, to capitalize upon her skill sets, and aid in performing in other areas such as reading, writing, and math and for reinforcement, as appropriate for her needs.

I reflected back to the number line with one through ten written on it in black marker. This was to teach Sierra ordinal numbers and counting. She was well past that. She knew her numbers up to thirty or more. The reason for other's not identifying with the underlying issue, was their negligence in understanding this, and looking at ways to support her learning. Because she didn't articulate it accurately, enough for it to be understood, or that she had compromised fine motor ability, didn't mean she didn't know it. It was up to the teacher to capitalize on techniques of engaging with her, to enhance communicating. It was crucial to pause and reflect on the subtle nuances, and gestures performed through parts of words and through movements. To listen closely, with an open mind and to slow down.

Sierra was my greatest teacher. Being encouraged to sit down without her body, organized prior to seat based earning was disadvantageous. It was up to the "team" to work with her most beneficially. Scheduling was difficult for them. So, O.T. and P.T. was scheduled when the teacher's had time. Their case-loads were large. I'm sure they were somewhat frustrated too. Charting goals in boxes held greater weight, then going outside the lines, and creating a diverse curriculum appropriate for a child with certain needs. However, we were a town with higher taxes. It was partly, why we moved to this town. We thought we'd receive better services. It seemed like survival of the fittest in this town. If you were willing to hire a top lawyer, you had a steep advantage. Still, it could take years. I wasn't used to this type of morality, at all. I wasn't going to understand it. It didn't resonate with me.

This goal-oriented approach applied to all disciplines, including art, music and lastly, gym. Gym was not part of what needed to be included as least restrictive in the manual for LRE. At our meeting at the school we met with her teacher, assistant to the special education supervisor, case manager, and the principal. It was shared that Sierra couldn't be integrated in gym with other "neuro-typical" peers. When I questioned why, I was told by the principal that it was because Sierra couldn't step on the red circle when asked. This was a just a few weeks into the school year. I was stunned.

I interjected with the fact that Sierra had an aide. This wasn't academic. It was a sport. It was something that Sierra deserved to be a part of. I shared how well Sierra was in gymnastics a couple of years back. Her instructor who was a professional dancer, also happened to be a teacher's aide in their school. She told us that out of all the children she worked with those few years at the Little Gym, that she never saw a child make such progress. Andy and I knew how strong-willed and intelligent she was. Although her motor planning was challenged, she was athletic. She needed to be with neuro-typical peers, as well. When we asked further about their reasoning for not allowing her in gym, the assistant supervisor of special education responded that the children in her class were her peer models. I was saddened because the philosophy was so segregated based upon ignorance or unjustly, fears. Differences are what makes us a more congenial, humble and compassionate society. It is a country to be united, not separated. It begins in the home and is more effective when it is carried out and reinforced at school.

Not My Life

Heck—-This was not my life! Not now. Not ever. Not for this Long!! Why things needed to have escalated or become so damn difficult, I couldn't wrap my head around it. My heart ached, as if particles of sandpaper were being impressed upon it, becoming rough and weathered on the surface. I didn't want to become hardened in such a granulated manner, where uncertainty governed. Inside of me, I was more forgiving, and these smoother areas would prevail. I was not cut out for this type of indignity. If it was about having a strong will, then, certainly, I was given the test of using it. If it was about any prospect of this being a testimony of my last life, then I was confident that this was it.

"Bring it on!" In those stark moments where I felt like I was hidden in the confinements of this inverted sand dune, I reminded myself of the courage within me. I made it this far. Part of me didn't—let me rephrase that, couldn't believe any of this. It was sink or swim. It tugged on this fight or flight response. Where was the middle? The not so much drama, you know—the easier, more forgiving path. A book I read, called "The Middle Place" was about a middle-aged woman who had cancer. She had two little girls and a loving husband. She had a close relationship with her mother and father, more so with her dad. She began looking at her life differently, with an understanding that they were getting older, and she might need to take care of them, too. She was faced with a life-threatening illness; cancer. She needed to take care of herself and her young children and now, her father who had cancer. It was about being in the middle of this place, feeling like a child still at heart, daddy's little girl, and a struggling mom with an illness. She had to be responsible, yet first to herself. It was about humility, commitment, sacrifice, and acceptance. It touched me in such a profound way. In those pre-Sierra days, when I was receiving messages to slow down and truly enjoy the moment, I reminded myself of the power, the ability, and the knowledge within.

With conviction I declared, "I can handle this!" With belief in myself, God, the angels, I could do this. My focused nature I put to good use. Yet, when I couldn't set something aside for a while, it often comprised my mind. I researched constantly. I wanted to find the best advocate, doctor, nurse, teacher and if I couldn't find them, I wasn't going to give up. I would heal my daughter. Like a cascading effect, I watched my little girl's health fading right before my very own eyes. All I could think about was saving her. The best way was to support her, in any way I could.

I continued to search. I shared my knowledge and opinions about what I firmly believed in, even IF, it was not acknowledged by others, in a more favorable way. It was not personal. Perhaps, I was a purple sheep, more unconventional than the mainstream. I reminded myself of the benefits of this, and that this was a good thing.

Being present with Sierra, following her lead, the world that she understood by joining with her, was essential for her growth process. Whether it be through gestures, sounds, or words—I would continue to listen.

We were designed of our own DNA's, our own body compositions, which are indeed, changeable over time. We all had different roles to play on this earth. That was where we united. We needed to embrace differences.

This was the way that all-natural disasters presented themselves. It would envelop, expand, and eventually crash. We had to crash before we could regain our momentum. Here, we emerged as a society, as we all had a responsibility, and a part in this. We each of us, mattered. Our children were the one's taking the fall. For now, this huge monster of a wave was emerging full speed ahead. I'd stand tall and let the waves descend. I watched Sierra soar, as she rode her wave with dignity and with grace.

Strength of Voice

I was driven to do away with the superficial suits many wore and were intrigued by. A façade to downplay something richer at the core. Whether you were wealthy, middle class, or poor, this seemed predominant in our society. Inside the walls of our schools, how much could one teach in these parameters led by a system that cared more about the superficiality of test scores for determining our intellect. Checking boxes for policies and state requirements was ineffective. Our children knew more than what was on the surface of being inundated with questions that would not bar them from understanding a greater scope of learning through experiences. Many teachers felt stuck in a lock and key method of teaching to these standards.

To those children in special needs classes, including learning disabled, communication challenged, auditory processing issues, autism, etc. I wanted to shout, "Color outside of the lines!" The bar was so uniformly set with everything being the exact shape and color, where one's imagination could not even remotely run WILD. The greater the children's challenges, it seemed the greater the restrictions were placed upon learning, in a more fluid and gentle way. Creativity needed to come to the forefront, and task analysis and conformity outside. It was an inside out approach.

To teach to the individual—Yes! As per one's IEP, Individualized Education Program that adhered to FAPE, Free and Appropriate Public Education developed back in 1973. Perhaps, this needed to be refined and more developed. To prompt with a stop and go response to elicit responses from children was jarring the body of its own innate ability to make decisions for oneself. It may take a few years, or more to acclimate into a range of adequate to more essential integrative concepts. To obtain information for goal charts for state mandated reasons was depriving our children of a real education. These tests were often designed for lucrative gains for companies that had political support. It was a win-win for them. Standardized tests to determine one's skills or aptitude for learning was often inaccurate. This would not conclude my daughter's ability to perform or predetermine the course of my daughter's life.

We were not all goldfish in a large aquarium. We were diverse learners. Sierra needed to be seen and heard for who she was. She had ideomotor apraxia, and it was more prominent than the autism label. She had pans and auto-immune responses that caused OCD and issues with language brought forth from the basal ganglia being affected. All this needed to be taken into consideration when learning. There were no real communication programs, except if you were deaf or hard of hearing. Apraxia was in a different area of the brain then autism. Three days a week of speech for a half an hour and an augmentative device would only prove effective if it was carried over in the classroom by the teacher and the aide, and the other therapists working with her. The numbers of children with more complex challenges was growing by the minute. We needed to take more of an invested interest with strategies unique to the individual. Schools needed more than one philosophy to support differences in the classrooms. We need dedicated teachers to be valued for their gifts and to have more programs to support them, as well as required training for aides to serve our children, more effectively. We needed trained nurses and doctors on staff, a real cohesive unit. That was the true calculation where the output could be seen with quality care and efficacy, increasing the value of our children's individual needs, and therefore, their future. It is our future.

Having "off" days accounted for variability in her performance. We needed to take into consideration the unique needs of the child. When Sierra was not being challenged or heard, anger and disappointment surged through me, sometimes as if I was about to burst. I would not give away my power, nor my ability to maintain a more peaceable state of being. Those rose-colored glasses I held, that had supported me in the rougher times, I had to take off. Even though in my fervent imagination, I could color almost anything. I needed to face reality. It would take a mountain, and we would move them.

I held the key necessary for my own self-growth and development. Today, I was living on the edge. Even if it was a jagged edge at that, it was okay. It was where I was at. The Jagged Edge of the Mountain. Jump! Jump into these waters! You can do it! Jump Sierra! Jump! You can do it! We will jump in it together!

Opening My Eyes More

I let go of some of the tightness. I reached for something like valerian root or ashwaghanda to temporarily alleviate any worries. I continued my quest for answers. Tirelessly researching, I rummaged through my cabinets to find the right supplements, herbs, oils, or vitamins. Often, I communicated with a very informed friend who had a son with special needs. I needed some relief, time to regroup. Although yoga was a savior for me attending at least, three days a week, having close friends who were genuine and compassionate was helpful. I welcomed people in my life who were genuine, and accepting of others, despite differences.

The tears came and went. The culprit of it was burning inside of me. Sierra was innocent, pure, kind, and beautiful. I would not be caught up in a web, a web of lies. As sensitive as I was, I was fair. I included people. I didn't avoid people or leave them out because of what they looked like, where they came from, or judge them because of their ability or performance, in intellectualizing.

My child's health was at stake, at risk, for something greater than the unclear diagnoses we were given. She needed a balance of proper nourishment, proper care, proper schooling, proper therapy, and proper treatment.

Where was our team? I went back to the basics, as in the comforts of my home, my safe and sound environment, the only place I could turn to. As I wrote, I turned to my artistry, and to my daughter. I turned to my family—the small family I had.

My desire for a close family member, one whom I felt acknowledged by, one who called me to ask if I was okay, or to find out how Sierra was doing, I always appreciated.

I searched for more answers. Andy wanted to see things, as facts, statistically proven. It took some time before he was able to see glimpses of things from a different perspective, a way that was not as scientifically sound. Not everything was so defined. Our picture-perfect world was imperfect. More than I ever, I knew we had to plunge in and explore other avenues.

Pulling Inwards
by Pulling out

It was December. It was cold outside. There was a coldness found within layers of ignorance inside of people. I grew tired of the fight. I wanted more for Sierra. And so, after careful thought and with Sierra's best interest in mind, I pulled her out of the contained environment she was in. It had little opportunity for self-growth, with seldom opportunities for inclusion. She would be home with me and venture out to different places for a more generalized learning experience. Sierra would make many of the calls, and I was attentive to her needs. I made some of the calls when Sierra needed to be guided and challenged more. We worked together as a team, as mother and child, two teachers or two students, learning from one another.

Art, music, creativity, speech, occupational therapy and music therapy were part of Sierra's daily activities. She could wake up without having to rush to get out of bed, especially when she could sometimes barely open her eyes. It was a difficult night, with regards to sleeping. At times, I'd get up, help clean herself, or give her a tubby. It took time. I wanted her to be in an environment where she could adjust and reacclimate, on her time.

A big challenge was having a supportive community of people that were more understanding and compassionate, regardless of one's abilities. It was isolating much of the time. I had no other children, besides my pup. We didn't have any young cousins. In addition, we lived on a street where children were hardly, seen playing outside. I welcomed a couple of children, however the playdates never happened. I supposed it was because children had friends from school and after school programs. Besides, as children got older, they adhered to a certain set of standards and held their own opinions. They learned from their parents, as well, and if they weren't open minded, children picked up on that. It was my quest to find a friend for Sierra nearby and other classes she'd enjoy.

It was very difficult to find programs for children with special needs, besides maybe one or two, and it didn't mean it was right for her. We tried a dance class which had too large an age span and too varied the diagnoses, that it proved to be rather chaotic in nature. It was also taught by a professional dancer, who delved right into watching her and following what she was doing, and quite rapidly. That wasn't working well for Sierra.

Sierra had speech and taekwondo on Saturdays, which was when another dance program was held, that I heard wonderful things about. Social skills groups were not advantageous to her because they organized these according to the amount of words expressed by each individual. Then, they would pair them up. When I had inquired about this a few times, I mentioned that Sierra was attentive and social, followed by having global apraxia which didn't mean she didn't have words. She had a lot of difficulty organizing the sounds for greater output. Sierra needed peers to play with and socialize with. My friend's children were involved in sports, academia, and other after school activities. I was growing more frustrated and tired. I wasn't sleeping as much. I never stopped researching on the web and making calls throughout my days.

As Sierra and I ventured out, I felt as though others thought that I was intentionally being disrespectful when she was crying or having a tantrum. Some watched and stared. Their mouths gaped open, while others avoided, and turned their heads. This required greater patience on my part, as I often thought this would be met with an empathic response from a kind soul.

Ideal or Real

Creatively driven and passionate about using our gifts to brighten our world with love and compassion, I realized that people from all nationalities, religions, and backgrounds were human beings who had the capacity to act with fear. We had a choice to allow those darker specs in or to welcome in the lighter side. I had either witnessed or been in the company of darkness at times. To attract the goodness in me and for the purpose of helping Sierra, I was determined to find that rare gemstone.

Time had been ticking. Where would Sierra be in terms of her development next year, three years from now, five years, and ten? I knew she was independent in so many ways, yet her motor planning and her communication were challenged. That brilliant mind of hers needed to be tended to, seen and heard.

An innovative person had stepped into our home when Sierra was six years old. We were given his number by a social worker who highly recommended him. She knew we were interested in the developmental model, DIRFloortime®. He modeled this methodology in a unique way, that was brought back to my attention from my yoga certification program a long time ago; slowing down, and noticing the subtle nuances, both verbally and non-verbally.

Frank arrived here one summer afternoon. Briskly, he walked up to our door, practically leaped into our home, shoes softly tossed off. He looked up at me, smiled and said," Hello", immediately followed by, "Where is She?" I pointed up the stairs, sort of stunned, as I followed close behind. He emerged into our daughter's bedroom, and immediately began playing with her. As she jumped, he did, too. As she made simple, happy glee like sounds and approximations of words, so did he. He connected with her, noticing the subtle nuances in her voice and mannerisms. His understanding nature was elicited in his attentiveness towards Sierra, with questions asked, slowly at a pace that she understood. He easily picked up Sierra's emotive forces in relation to her communication. He remained present on an emotional level, as he altered his tone, pitch and rhythm to meet her where she was at.

The day he walked out that door I knew, there would be more of something. Something I couldn't quite put my finger on it. After a couple of sessions, I shared with him that one session was worth more than a hundred speech sessions. He thanked me, rather humbly. Sierra was verbalizing and requesting more. He was non-judgmental, accepting differences. He was a welcoming friend. He genuinely appeared to enjoy his work.

I sat down at my laptop and did a search on in his name. I came across a story he created, written like an old century poet. As I read further, I couldn't believe it paralleled a metaphysical story I had worked on, in prior years. His ever-flowing words were so eloquently put. I discovered his website that entailed information about his developmental approach. I reached out to him in several texts, as I was interested in any thoughts and ideas about how I could help Sierra. I never met anyone so brilliantly articulate and knowledgeable about child development. I felt more hopeful than I had been since Sierra had been diagnosed with these challenges. He seemed so eager and interested in supporting her, and in guiding me, as her mother.

He read up on Son-Rise®, a program he knew I was quite familiar with, as I had shared my knowledge of the technique with him. I had watched many videos on the approach. I had found out about it, as years before, I took a class at the Option Institute called, "Happiness is a Choice". The founders of the program were Barry Neil and Samahria Lyte Kaufman. They had a son named Raun who was diagnosed with severe autism. They were told by the experts in this field that he would need to "be institutionalized with a "hopeless, life-long condition". (Autism Treatment Center of America). They were determined to work with him with every ounce of love in them, by accepting him and being present with him, not defining him as anything less than a beautiful intelligent, insightful, and very capable child. They'd join in with him, in a playful and compassionate way. With an insurmountable amount of courage and unconditional love, they tirelessly worked with him day in and day out. They understood that it was about making connections and building from that, as they listened in to what his needs were and honored, where he was at. If he spinned plates, so did he. If he rocked, so did they. They encouraged him through imitation, and song, and introduced speech. They challenged him and didn't give up. Raun became an interactive, social and highly verbal, child. He had lost his diagnoses of autism and his I.Q. which was once a thirty, became a near genius I.Q. He graduated from Brown College with a degree in Biomedical Ethics. He became a mentor for many, teaching about the Son-Rise® program, and the Option Process® throughout the world.

I applied this technique when we first found out about Sierra's challenges. Quickly, I put this into practice. She became more fluid in terms of movement, more attentive and interactive. I used puppets and music, played hide and seek, as I witnessed new awakenings. I saw in her eyes and in her affect, a greater awareness. I followed her lead, imitating her movements, and I joined in with her.

When Frank came into our lives with a unique understanding of the significance of the space in between the words, and the knowledge of the social emotional aspects underlying what was spoken, I was so very appreciative of this. It put a spark back into my life, as he grasped the concept with such ease and would, indeed help her. He confided in me that it was refreshing to speak with me, someone with a similar philosophy who could appreciate the ideas he valued, expressed, taught, and shared. He let me know that I understood the essential concepts rather well ,and quickly.

It gave me such hope, as he got it. It was something simple and meaningful. Having similar interests in health and psychology, and having a creative outlet in poetry, it was as though I found a life-long friend. I felt dampened by a society that didn't interpret communication in this way. Now, I found someone who understood both me and my daughter.

He had all the pieces to help Sierra integrate; However, due to unforeseen circumstances, we had to cease contact. I knew this person with the philosophy he held, arrived here to show us something profound. The way he understood the silence between the sounds, the spaces in between the words, to listen and assimilate information and to guide us, was a significant part of helping Sierra give quality to her voice—To express herself more and be confident in it.

This experience made me shine and grow dim, coincidingly. I reached out to others with a floortime background. There weren't many who specialized in this, at least in our county. Some had full time jobs, others resided further away. The couple of therapists that I interviewed didn't connect with Sierra in the same way. I realized that Frank wasn't the ideal. He was real.

Choosing to Rise Above

I continued to rise above the chitter-chatter in my mind and not believe all the hype of the philosophies that weren't as effective. I needed to figure out our next steps. In between the days that were fiercely difficult, I reflected back to the past.

The true admiration I had for Frank, the way he would put his thoughts into form, and understood the development of language in a social context. He drew out information from a very unique and insightful psychological perspective. I would continue to work with Sierra in my way. I was learning so much. Some experiences were clearer reflections for me, a mirror for me, to look deeper.

There were days I sank into an abyss like state. My husband was suffering as well. Both individually, and as a family, we were coming apart at the seams. On this roller coaster ride, I began to look at the threads of us, of our family.

Family time—Andy's cousins lived just a few miles away from us. They were kind, thoughtful and loving to Sierra. On some Sundays, I ventured out and joined Andy and Sierra in their daily outing at Cookie, a city like French gourmet café in our town. Michael, our cousin would join us for breakfast sometimes. Michael's sister, Hannah, had a lot of activities she participated in such as acting, dance, and ballet. Their mom Abigail was busy working or taking Hannah to auditions in the city, or simply, being a mom. Dan, their dad was around sometimes. There were long weekends for him that consisted of travel hockey, etc. Sierra greatly enjoy spending time with them. She was enamored by her big cousin Hannah, as she watched her put on makeup and played in her room. She loved giving Hannah and Michael big hugs. She would put her arm around Michael during the time they hung out together. He'd joke around with her and was quite playful in his adoring and loving way, and sat alongside her, while he played his video games.

Grandma and Grandpa visited every three or four weeks. They were kind to Sierra and interested in her. My dad would get on the floor with her, as she did puzzles, or sing to her, while tickling her toes. He sang, "This Little Piggy" almost every time. I envisioned him continuing with this, when she was older. Just because, that was my dad with good intentions. We visited grandma and grandpa sporadically. As most parents can attest to, when you have young children, packing for the day can be quite a tedious and time-consuming task. Time at their home meant that they might find a few leaves missing, or sand on the floor from the beach, etc. One plant was my Great Grandmothers," Old Nanny Glick's". I had mixed emotions about going there, as I didn't want to upset my parents. They would say it's okay, but I knew inside it bothered them.

My parents were good to Sierra and very giving to us. They were thoughtful, brought her clothes, toys, or books and were generous on birthdays and holidays. They were responsible and tried to do what was right. The precious time spent together, I very much appreciated.

I wished I could have saved my parents from some trips to the doctor. They went often. They went to more traditional doctors and we went the alternative route, with some traditional as well. I didn't want to cause them any more worry. Our little family was different than what we had thought. It was okay.

One person I would have loved to be closer to was, my sister. Jill lived in Colorado with her husband. Their son, my nephew, Eli, was four years older than Sierra. Although we had some different philosophies, I hoped we could find a more even way of communicating with each other. When Jill had an opinion and I didn't agree, she often retaliated. There were times, it was essential for me to be heard and validated, even if she didn't agree. It wasn't that I wasn't listening to her advice. I valued her opinions on some matters, yet there were others I didn't adhere to. Some were more intimate in scope, and not to be judged. Our closeness as sisters had become as vast as our distance within a geographical location. I hoped one day that would change, and we would shed the past, and honor one another, as individuals, and as sisters.

My husband was there for our family, as much as he could be. After his long tiresome days of work at a bank he worked at for over twenty-six years and riding home on a bus home, sometimes in traffic, it was a stretch to discuss much afterwards. Time was limited during the week. On the weekends, he was always there for her tending to her needs. I was very appreciative of all he did. He loved his special moments with Sierra, whether it was playing with her, giving her tubbies, tucking her in, or dancing with her. He enjoyed being her dad.

Days Out Away
from Home

Oh, the places we'd go. It was like Dr. Seuss's pictures having different avenues to explore, including navigating through those dark places to come into the light. What would happen as we moved through the course of our day into unknown territories, being okay with what would happen next? We had easier days, and those much more difficult. We ventured out and explored at our own pace. Sierra's curiosity was insatiable. When she felt better and something sparked her interest, she let me know, in various ways. She often reached over and kissed my forehead, smiled at me, looking me right in the eyes, and laugh. She walked with an extra jig in her step, and would sometimes, take my hand and run with me. Sierra loved animals. We went to a local park in northern NJ, about a fifteen-minute drive from here. It was a small zoo that Sierra enjoyed. Some of the cages were smaller in size which I couldn't understand the reasoning for such contained spaces. However, it was an educational experience. They tried to provide as natural an environment, as they could. I would read some of the excerpts on the signs containing information about their backgrounds and histories of how they evolved. The park had a small train that circled around it, along with a carousel ride.

One issue was use of a bathroom and that of a clean one. Sierra was wearing pull ups. I had my purifier close by in my pockets, which I sprayed often at the zoo. I was cautious about Sierra developing symptoms, catching another bacteria, virus, or parasites or whatever she might pick up. I would change her in the back seat of our car. I hovered inside the doorway that was open just enough to provide space to help Sierra out. I tried not to get too impatient with myself, as I was careful of others nearby, in the process. Sierra was getting older and bigger in size. I watched mothers with their babies, as they changed them in the back of their trunks, the days when that was typical of a child's development.

I tried not to well up inside, yet appreciate the little things, especially knowing that they happen in increments, not always defined or seen.

I watched children saying, "no" or telling or pointing to their parent something they were curious about, "Look mommy, over there, a tiger, etc." Some parents paid little attention, as they were accustomed to hearing them, I suppose. It opened me up for greater acknowledgement in the subtleties of life. I could see more of the essentials and the beauty of those small miracles.

After the zoo, and on many other days, we went out for lunch. One of our go to places was Whole Foods as well as a co-op. When the days were warmer, we enjoyed going to the co-op and ate outside. There were days Sierra experienced greater hyperactivity.

Other days were calmer in temperament. At the little buffet, we picked up her favorite barbecue chicken and some brown rice. This was one of Sierra's favorite meals, as well as, onion soup. Her preferences changed, as she was a child. She loved flavorful foods with a lot of spices. I did, as well. I liked spiced foods, but not spicy. At times, it was challenging to pick up something for myself, as Sierra could be moving about quickly, lifting open a container or two, or touching cookies, donuts, breads or other foods. Sometimes, she would run upstairs. I always wanted to make sure she was safe. Protecting others from their own insecurities, was not my problem. I smiled and made lighter of things sometimes, but there were days that it was significantly harder. As I stood at the cashier's line, I hoped that the laidback natures of the cashiers might quicken their pace. One day at the co-op, a twenty-ish something boy said, "She's got a mind of her own." I responded with, "Yes! She surely does."

One day as we were shopping at Whole Foods in another town, Sierra started screaming, just as we entered. Concerned, I'd ask her, what had happened. Sometimes, her cries might elevate louder, and then I often said, "Sierra—What can I do to help you?" She might relax, or maybe, not. Then it might escalate. This one particular day, many eyes were situated towards us. I screamed alongside Sierra, for just a second or two. Actually, it was somewhat relieving. I shrugged my shoulders and responded in a soft, matter of fact tone, "Anyone have a problem?" Partially, under my breath I muttered, "She's just being herself. She's a child." Not one person came over to ask, "Are you okay?" "Is there anything I can do to help you?" In a different place, a different town, a different city, or state, or country, or just maybe, a different world. That is what

I surmised at that moment and other times, "Why not offer a kind word, a simple smile, or a reassuring look? It made all the difference.

Summertime—
The Beach

Sierra's favorite place was being immersed in a place of comfort the sands, the waters, the warmth of the sun. What better place, than the beach. Sierra enjoyed going to the YMCA's manmade beach. It was clean. How she loved the feeling of those soft granules of sands upon my feet. We would drive from Oakland, only about ten minutes from our home to get there. I packed up our gear—towels, shovels, and pails, and snacks in our royal blue Subaru. We arrived safely. Before we got out, I made sure Sierra's swimmies were dry. If they weren't, I'd change her in the car.

Sierra would be smiling from ear to ear. I tried not to be worried about changing her, but I did what I had to, and often, in the car. Going into the outdoor bathroom's there was too gross to think about. Though, I ventured in there a couple of times, it hadn't been very forgiving in terms of cleanliness. Andy would take her into the men's room on the weekends. Sierra was growing older though, and it was different when she was three, four or five for that matter.

Sierra loved the beach. She was so excited to be there, as she placed her petite feet into the grooves on the hot sands. She happily walked and rather quickly as she made her way in, and sometimes ran towards the water. I was thrilled to see that she enjoyed it so much, the little things. I'd remind Sierra—First, we needed to take off our clothing as we also unpacked our belongings. I had this large Velcro nylon blanket that was like a shoulder bag, and unfolded at the seams, I'd remove this fast. It seemed milliseconds before Sierra moved, swiftly towards the water. Again, I was so happy for her, however I couldn't move as quickly. I enjoyed the intimate moments we shared together. It would have been wonderful to have another person to converse with or having another to help us out, would have been beneficial. I wanted to slow down, for my own sake, for Sierra's sake.

I ran with Sierra to the shoreline. Sierra dipped her legs in. She cautiously walked in and out. Then, after a little while, plummet right in. There was a large fountain a little further out from the shore line. She walked around it, and then when she was ready, got right in it. She enjoyed the thrill of dipping her whole head in. There's my fish, I would think. I smiled inside. We sang simple songs. In brief interludes, I would hear her sweet voice. "Go, Mommy, more, or again."

As I pulled her round and round, Sierra would let out a belly laugh. It was contagious. It brought warmth to my heart. Sometimes, I craved more interaction with another and wanted a little friend for Sierra. I hoped a little girl would come over to Sierra and play with her. Maybe, one day, I thought. So, she had a learning challenge. So, her words were muffled, or unclear. She was sweet and kind.

We came out of the water and found our way towards our large blanket. Sierra had her eye on the snack bag, as soon as we sat down. I took out our towels and wrapped Sierra up. Then, I encouraged her to walk towards the house where the outside showers were, as I wanted to wash the chlorine and anything from the lake off her body. When we returned, we relaxed for a bit and chowed down on some fruits, pretzels, and crackers. Visiting there a few times a week was well worth the trip. It was a place Sierra enjoyed. I welcomed in the sunshine.

Getting Sierra Healthy—
A New School for
Continued Learning

I wrote countless emails to our school district about finding the right placement for Sierra's needs. We hired a lawyer through my husband's company. She was not a special needs lawyer though, interested in helping us. She seemed intelligent and spoke with confidence and articulated her thoughts well. However, during mediation where we met with the team from our district, her boldness and her ability to speak her thoughts was not apparent. She sided with the mediator when it came to the right model for Sierra, which the team agreed upon, as ABA.

Even though I had several professional letters stating this was not the right methodology for Sierra, I had to work within the parameters of what the school board members and team decided upon as appropriate. They sent me a list of schools for Sierra. I remained within the scope of ABA, searching tirelessly for the right teacher. My dear friend shared with me about this one magnet school. She knew of two parents who boasted about how great the program was. It was close to New York City and was more culturally savvy, I thought. I met with the behaviorist and an experienced long-standing teacher in one of their schools. After visiting, I felt very much at ease that there would be ample opportunities for Sierra. There were several special education classes and inclusion beginning with specials in art, music, gym, and recess. It was determined that one particular educator would be a great fit. As I looked her name up in the school's directory, I noticed that she had a floortime background, and had worked at the Marcus Program. Perhaps, this was divine timing. When I met with her, our case manager, and social worker, we all agreed it was appropriate. Sierra would be in a self-contained center-based ABA program.

Sierra would be considered a first grader, as she was six years of age now. I was so excited she was in good hands with a welcoming and supportive staff.

Banalli Blvd.

The drive to Banalli Boulevard was a fourteen-mile distance without traffic. It was like city driving. Narrowed highways, many lights, and one very long stretch of time waiting for a five-minute dinner light to turn green.

We listened to a wide array of music. Music for aardvarks, Music Together, Sting, Billy Joel, Jewel, and Sarah McLachlan, to Sirius, and You tube with James Bay, Keisha, Kelly Clarkson, Sheryl Crowe, and others. During our trip, I asked Sierra I'd offer her choices, as I'd show her a couple of cd's in the midst of traffic, doing my best to make her ride a pleasurable one. Also, I asked her if she'd like some snacks. It wasn't the easiest of routes, however it was the place I chose for Sierra to attend school.

The teacher I handpicked for this coming school year had moved to Minnesota. A newly appointed teacher was hired to replace her role as a teacher. During our meeting with the Director of Special Education, inquisitively and in anticipation asked, "Do you think she's a good fit for Sierra's needs?" She responded that she had a similar background to the former teacher with regards to her skills in teaching. She was knowledgeable in a multisensory approach called, Orton Gillingham. In my mind, I thought that's fine on paper. More importantly, was the understanding of how she would bring out the knowledge to the forefront, to bridge the gap between what a child knows and elicit valuable information from them. Would she encourage and support the children's interests, while instilling a love of learning?

We decided to go forward, as we had committed to being there, and school was starting in a couple of weeks. After starting school, when weeks had passed, I hadn't received any notes on Sierra's day in her logbook. There was no homework sent home either. There was nothing presented to me to understand what was being taught in the classroom. I wanted to support Sierra at home to reinforce learning, and in being complementary to help her with generalizing concepts.

My biggest concern was in utilizing ABA strategies, as a priority, over the individual needs of our child. Sierra would benefit from a teacher who was warm, intuitive, skilled and creative. Of most importance was having that social emotional approach, engaging with the child, watching for subtle cues, and building upon each small increment. Making inferences, understanding when to move forward and back, and challenging through a technique such as floortime. At least, in terms of building connections, by establishing rapport first, and leading into practical to more functional or abstract thinking for higher problem-solving skills to occur. Taking into strong consideration a child's interests was key.

Because it was difficult for Sierra to communicate with me about her day, it was essential that I received feedback from the teacher and the therapists on a daily basis. Unfortunately, the feedback had been minimal. I learned about what Sierra ate or didn't eat, and toileting. There was information about some things they worked on. I wanted to know more about Sierra's daily interactions, and what concepts she worked on, and homework to reinforce that at home. I wanted to let Sierra know that I was a part of her school day and converse with her about it. What was more challenging, was the little interaction I had with other parents, as we lived a good distance from one another, about thirty or more minutes away. I hadn't been involved in the community attending PTA meetings or others. Also, several parents spoke a different language. Spanish was some of the parent's primary language. I reached out via phone and as I acquired a middle school skill level, I used it to the best of my ability. It was discouraged to give out numbers or emails from the teachers. I gave our number to them, to give to the parents, but hadn't received an email, text, or a call, up until this past year. You can bet, I was thrilled to interact and share with a classmate's mother.

It was like we were hidden under a book, instead of being included within the threads of it, as part of a team. Perhaps, a different methodology wasn't understood, but where was the quality of respect, in regards for parent contact, and a mother who appreciated learning and teaching her child. I wanted to pull her out, however Andy was not in favor of homeschooling. I wasn't either, in part, as I knew the demands that I would place upon myself, in teaching her optimally, and in finding the right therapists and children for Sierra to play with on a daily basis. Plus, we were limited in the number of hours allotted for speech and occupational therapy and other practitioners, regarding insurance coverage.

Too Much of Something

Sierra began over utilizing the word "boo". It increased for days. She doesn't script or typically, repeat words. Anne, Sierra's speech therapist, sent home what she referred as these "noisy books". I opened one up to discover that the word "Boo" was on every other page. Having a severe apraxia component, she was motivated by being praised for her attempts at articulating words, and phrases. Sierra was excited to say, "Boo!" Obviously, it was a lesson that was given to her daily and I assumed it was valued or rewarded quite frequently. Previously, we spoke to the school and emphasized how important a global approach was for Sierra. It would aid her in her receptive and expressive language and support her in generalizing ideas.

It took us about two months or more to unravel her overreliance on this word. I incorporated it when we played peek-a-boo, alongside her, as I pretended to be a ghost. I aimed at desensitizing its use, and that there would be a more comprehensive understanding of it. I knew upon receiving the second noisy book, when Sierra had repeated another word, what this was attributed to. I was baffled by the reasoning that Anne was using such an ineffective approach. I had hoped that she would move on from utilizing this method as a single point of interest, within their sessions.

I made an appointment with Anne to discuss this. When I conveyed to her my concerns, she was almost silent. This type of depersonalization with a response like that, appeared odd. I approached her rather humbly, and with concern. I hoped for greater input as in brainstorming with her; even though, I wasn't a speech therapist. I was creative, and an educator, and I was willing to sharing what I could, in terms of utilizing a more global approach, including a game, dolls, puppets, etc. I spoke about integrating more information within the extent of generalizing the story. I emphasized that the noisy books were black and white, so it would have been advantageous to apply color, or have Sierra use crayons or pastels. This was a reward in itself as it elicited an interaction to build confidence. It supported fine motor development, as well.

This was not personal. It was about helping my daughter to learn effectively, in a way that worked for her individual needs. Due to her reticent nature I couldn't fathom continuing in this way.

Not long after, we requested a change in speech therapists with another one in the school that had more years of experience. We had a meeting with her and a couple of other staff members. We wanted so much to be part of a team to benefit Sierra. We shared with her about Sierra in terms of speech, incorporating play and socialization. She seemed interested and willing to discover more about Sierra. I shared I'd be very appreciative if she could send me some emails on the sessions. A simple note to tell me how she's doing with supplementary tools that I could carry over at home. I received a couple of emails. Nearing the end of the year, we received information that she would be retiring. Perhaps, the upcoming speech therapist would provide us with greater communication.

End of the Year—
Breaking the Silence

We had a meeting with an outside speech therapist and occupational therapist, as hired by my home school district. The speech therapist had gone several times to implement this augmentative device, and trained Sierra's teachers about its functions. These two women came to the school over the course of many months. They tested Sierra in a variety of areas relating to the scope of speech and occupational therapy. At the end of the year, I met with our case manager, and the speech and occupational therapist.

The speech therapist shared that Sierra was performing well with one of the programs they had decided upon for the augmentative device. She was able to utilize a multitude of pictures with words on it without a problem. When I asked about the implementation of it in the classroom, and if they were using it effectively, she shared that they were, yet didn't feel as though Sierra was being challenged enough, overall by her teacher. The speech therapist continued to express that she was much more capable in learning concepts than the materials presented to her.

I did my absolute best to reach out to the team there including the behaviorist, Lila. Lila was the most responsive. She was bubbly, innovative, and more child directed in her approach. She didn't say much about the techniques the teacher was using, however was open to helping Sierra in the best way she could.

I had the opportunity to come in and observe a session. Sierra was at a large wipe board. There was a circle drawn on the top, a triangle below it, and under that a square. She was instructed to draw a couple of shapes two times each on a smart board. I couldn't imagine what Sierra felt inside. It was a flat board with nothing enticing to encourage her to want to participate in this. In addition, it was difficult for her to draw the triangle and square. Eventually, Sierra plopped herself down on the floor and cried. The teacher asked Sierra what had happened. The behaviorist, Lila was present engaging with her in a natural way, listening to her needs, attending to her subtle cues, and offering her some other choices.

It greatly concerned me that there was little proactivity in assisting Sierra in making something productive and fun with it. Perhaps, cutting out circles for a snowman, a triangle for a hat, and squares for buttons. Applying different materials such as buttons, felt, paint, etc. Maybe, using clay to create the shapes, seeing this was tougher for her, and offering her choices. Offering a way to generalize the concepts could have proved to be more satisfactory. It was difficult to leave. I gave Sierra a kiss goodbye and rubbed her heart. She tugged onto me. I gave her a butterfly kiss upon her lashes and nodded my head to her, letting her know I understood. She gave me a little smile.

I called a team meeting. At our meeting, we discussed options for the following year. We were offered the opportunity to be placed in Ms. Daniel's classroom. It was a more advanced class. We met with Ms. Daniel's that summer who had about sixteen years of experience there. She was empathic and interested in providing Sierra with options to assist her in learning new skills in a more generalized way. We discussed the necessity for Sierra's aide to give her more space, in order for her to grow, utilize, and develop independent skills. Sierra wanted to learn and had great potential. She needed the proper support and feedback. She was open to speaking with us in an ongoing manner. We emphasized that Sierra needed a complementary approach that included the teacher, the therapists, and our family working together.

Digging Deeper

The year had begun. Off she went like a race horse. I was ready for Sierra to begin, again. I hoped this was a better year for her, both academically and socially. Four boys in her class, all began with an "A". Three of them had similar names, all different derivatives of the name Andy. It was her dad's name, too. The one name that was different, also started with an "A". It was kind of humorous. We were thrilled that the teacher had experience and was open to other methods with a naturalistic teaching style.

There were a lot of questions and concerns that Sierra had new topics presented to her to acquire and assimilate with existing information. In that brilliant mind of hers, I hoped she'd flourish there. With expressive language issues and fine motor challenges, teacher's and therapists needed to be intuitive, skilled and confident enough to obtain information from her in creative ways, and to continue to challenge her.

The teacher seemed, genuinely interested in Sierra. As the year progressed, I noticed some worksheets sent home and very little homework. I asked for homework since last year, and to send home reinforcement for expanding on thematic units and for learning concepts covered in class. It could help Sierra in generalizing, along with other pertinent skills.

One day I came in to drop Sierra off. I asked if Ms. Daniel's could offer any information on what the occupational therapist was working on. She shrugged her shoulders and confided to me that she didn't know. My heart sank. Where was the team approach? There were five children in Sierra's class. I tried not to let frustration get the best of me. I responded with, "Can you ask her?" While I understood the therapists were swamped with a large caseload, there were some things that needed to be discussed and carried over in class, and in therapies. Ms. Daniel's showed compassion and seemed somewhat interested in what I was sharing. When I saw her teacher at pickup—"Sierra ate all of her raspberries, soup, and chick peas." "Sierra was happy today." "Sierra didn't have a great day." I knew it was pick up time and difficult to talk. It just seemed like, I always heard about what she ate and her emotions. When situations arose in the class, or when they were doing activities I wanted to know, "What did you as the teacher do to support Sierra?" "How did you intervene?" "How did Sierra respond to this?" I was hoping for more input and notes from the therapists. Mostly, they were limited in scope.

I was also concerned about Sierra's aide and if she was being flexible enough for her needs. She was lovely, a grandmother, about seventy-five years old. She seemed to care a lot about Sierra. I wasn't certain if having her as a one-one aide was going to support greater learning. Ms. Daniel's shared that the aide needed to give her more space, emphasizing that it was important for her independent skills. More than half the year had passed.

Soon after, I spoke with Ms. Daniel's about having more language support for Sierra. Maybe, a different method or perhaps, another program. She had asked me what a language school would look like in terms of supporting Sierra. It would always be a cohesive approach where the subject matter was woven into the course of the day. This was a more positive use of repetition in a global way. It was necessary to be humble and be open in trying new ways. If something did or didn't work, to discuss and communicate and work as a team, and to be transparent about it. To work with Sierra moment to moment, and reflect on this, and over time, we could see what would manifest. To know that an IPAD was not a substitute for her learning. To know that person-alization came from back and forth reciprocity with respect and with belief in another. This was an effective way for encouraging her to communicate.

Because Sierra's difficulty in motor planning inhibited her speech production, and more fluidly, she needed movement and not a static way of teaching. Challenging her when it was not a tabulated goal that she already knew, was essential. Doing away with this labeling of worksheets, and coloring within the lines. This was not self-expression. It was what I refer to as, "busy work". Sierra was in a special education class. Teach to her individual needs. Perhaps, larger scale paper and two and three dimensional, mediums to assist her with her gross motor and fine motor skills.

Breathe and s-l-o-w down. Simply, have fun. There seemed to be this constant pressure to perform. When a child wasn't achieving enough, according to standards that were not individualized due to compromises in their systems, don't give up on them. Expand the scope of learning. What could we, as teachers do to make a positive change in a child's life? Listen! We all had something to work with, not against ourselves, and not with flat sheets of paper.

In addition, I heard this phrase, multiple times—"When Sierra's ready". One time more recently, when I requested a dyad with another child, preferably with a girl in occupational therapy. Sierra wasn't given enough and with very little opportunities for integrating and socializing, especially with other little girls. The O.T. couldn't provide Sierra with an opportunity to bring in another child, preferably a girl to play with during a session. Later, I found out that since it was a first and second grade school, that there weren't many other little girls who received O.T. This was a little more comforting than the comment, "When she's ready."

Potty Time

Ms. Daniel's continued to use a timer in order to build the understanding as to when to use the bathroom. "What a great concept!" I suppose that is what mother nature wanted to do when she designed our precious bodies to be dictated and driven by a ticking object to decide for us when our next trip to the bathroom would be! I had shared with her teacher that we had a nationally expert potty trainer in our home, however that didn't seem to be enough to do away with this method. It was the same type of programming, held as part of ABA. If we throw her a bone, like a lollipop for a reward, she'll definitely use the bathroom. I hadn't known that Ms. Daniel's had been giving Sierra lollipops, as a reward each time she went. This was practically, every day. I found this out, when I came into the classroom and saw a new bag of "healthy" cane syrup filled pops in her hand. It was to reinforce this concept. I had given her a bag of these, and asked her to give it to her infrequently, along with other toys, games, etc.

September rolled by, then October, and November. Her teacher stated, "Sierra is getting it, however she doesn't go all the time, and she's not requesting it." Why on earth would she request it when she had a timer to do that for her! It could not dictate to her body to readjust itself, to have to urinate according to when it went off, every twenty or so, minutes.

During the month of February, I walked into the classroom. I was invited in when dropping Sierra off and coming in late that morning. Ms. Sandy whisked Sierra into the bathroom. She barely had her coat off after a long drive that morning of about forty-five minutes. It was advantageous to have the bathroom in the classroom with quicker access, perhaps a safer space, and with less children utilizing it.

I heard Sierra crying. I opened the door just a little bit, and saw that Ms. Sandy was holding Sierra's wrists. I quickly disengaged her hands, as I knew Sierra was getting frustrated. Sierra needed to get off of it. Sierra's feet also didn't touch the floor, so there wasn't any grounding force for her to have more control. She stated it was because Sierra was getting upset and she didn't want her to get hurt. I didn't understand this. Also, she shared that she had already urinated. What she needed was to get up from the toilet.

Ms. Daniel's agreed with me, followed by, "Ms. Sandy has her own mind". She mentioned to me that she requested Ms. Sandy to step back a little to allow Sierra more space. I was left with a disparaging feeling in my heart.

I reached out to my district requesting to see other schools. One that was more appropriate with meeting Sierra's needs, for her having a communication disorder. I wanted better support for her. I was reaching for straws. I felt like I was in a ditch, in this inverted sand castle on a desert island. Part of me wanted to stay inside and the other wanted to find a way out. I saw a ladder adjacent to me. I was not going to give up! With my hand on the ladder, I would take steps.

Ms. Daniel's shared with me one day, later that February, that she did away with the timer. As I picked her up from school by my car, she let me know that she hadn't requested to use the bathroom. I responded with, "It's day number one and without a timer." Her body and mind needed time to adjust, and a new way of approaching it, relying more upon her body, and not an inanimate object to direct her body to lead. Sierra was the Leader. She was responsible for her own timing—Not a timer. Not the lollipops. Not Ms. Sandy. No one and no thing, except SIERRA!

That day I came home with Sierra. She was having a hard time sitting with me for even short periods of time. It was becoming more habitual, this pattern. What was I to do? My little girl was being swallowed up by a system that wasn't working for her. She constantly needed to be touched, to lick her books, and rip them, for months now. This was how she was reacclimating. I felt like dying. That night, I was in the shower. As I let the water pass over me, it was as if I was washing everything off of me; the good, the bad and the ugly. I cried out, "Go to Hell!", as I pounded the marbled wall. As I stood behind that shower door, I yelled out for answers, for anything that could help her. I wanted us to live and just be, with normalcy in our lives in a place that was more accepting, understanding, and loving.

Shonishin and NAET

E very Thursday, I picked Sierra up from school to take her to see a woman who was a Licensed Acupuncturist, with training in shonishin and NAET. Shonishin was a needle free form of acupuncture for children with low immune function or problems with blood cells. Small metal tools were used to scratch, tap, and brush on the skin over acupuncture pathways. Its purpose was to stimulate the body, bringing it back in balance.

It was about a half hour drive to see Tamar, the acupuncturist. She had expertise in working with children with different types of needs. We had been on a waiting list, and she was able to get us in earlier, then expected. Tamar was a caring individual who was attentive and interested in finding solutions for Sierra's needs in terms of healing. Sierra would lay on the table most of time, and sometimes, Tamar worked with her on the large mat on the floor. She would take out the shonishin instruments, each one of different metal. Tamar shared that Sierra had a lot of excess heat in her body, and her arm would often turn bright red when she used the instruments. It meant she had a lot of qi (yang) energy in her body. She would brush this over her several times, on different acupuncture points related to specific organs of the body.

Tamar also utilized NAET (Nambudripads Allergy Elimination Technique). It is a form of alternative medicine that treats allergies and related issues. She used a vial with a certain substance in it. It would hopefully, desensitize her to whatever she was allergic or sensitive to. Tamar used kinesiology to test for various allergens. If Sierra tested positive to any of them, she'd do a certain type of treatment holding the vials with my hand on Sierra's skin as a neutral party to test to see if Sierra had a reaction to it. If she did, Sierra would need to refrain from being in contact with the allergen for a twenty-four hour period. Tamar also eliminated any harmful effects vaccines, as part of this process, later down the line, after others needed to be done to clear the system.

Typically, this took about forty-five minutes. Sierra was a real trooper for going.

Some days were easier than others. Sierra often leaked through her pull-up; as I sensed she was nervous or over excited about being there. I had reservations, however I believed it could be something that could really help her.

Tamar was hopeful. She would do research outside of this, attending workshops, and utilized some other approaches to help Sierra express more. This wasn't an area that was seen as being more effective, to the mainstream. I believed it aided in calming and focusing. After a year, we decided we would move on. Tamar was very supportive and dedicated. She wished us well. We did the same.

Growing—Healing—Learning

Finding that balance. What to focus on next? It came in increments. It was like waiting for a watched pot to boil. I needed to slow down, turn down the heat, cool off, and regain my momentum.

I needed to find that needle in a haystack. My husband had gotten bell's palsy. He was also suffering from a blocked artery in his heart. Perhaps, a vacation was necessary. Our piggy bank was running low. Instead, we found something else, well needed. It was a place situated in another country. It would not be surf and sand. It would be healing, however. It wasn't a quick fix, but a step in the right direction.

Revisiting Stem Cells

We were interested in the prospect of having Sierra receiving umbilical cord stem cells again. This time it was from a donor. I was on a face book site, dedicated to learning about and sharing information about stem cells. Many families were heading to Panama Stem Cell Institute to receive these sacred cells. These were families of children with neurological challenges, including the over labeled and broadminded term, autism. Basically, the numbers of ill children were growing that had compromised immune systems. I didn't care what you called it, I wanted Sierra to be treated with the right protocol, and bio-physiological treatment that was going to heal her on her path to recovery.

Sierra's greatest challenge according to her neurologist early on, was her speech. He shared what was disrupting or off setting it more so, was her nervous system, sensory, etc. Sierra needed a language-based program that would incorporate movement. Because that wasn't something that existed, except in one pre-school, the Marcus Center Program, it had to be created or at least, modified.

At this point, we had to supplement with therapies and continue our search to redefine and think out of the box with a more global perspective. Stem cells were a part of this solution, as our next venture. Then, putting together a program as best we could a program to meet Sierra needs in whatever school Sierra was at. Each year, I prayed that Sierra would have skilled and empathic teachers. One who had an open mind, one who would listen, and one who would understand that Sierra had auto-immune issues, with a variability. It wasn't just a behavior that could be extinguished with a reward. On days she didn't feel as well, provide her with more space, and create as supportive an environment as you could. If she was really not feeling well, she needed to be sent home.

I was reminded that shortly after receiving stem cell treatment at Duke, Sierra had similar symptomologies that brought on her pans/pandas symptoms. Dr. M., the neurologist diagnosed her with a high probability of having this. Pans was like Pandas in that viruses attacked antibodies and saw them as invaders. Certain viruses we tested Sierra for. There were so many to test for, so we really didn't know besides mycoplasma pneumonia, what other one's aggravated her system.

When we attended a meeting with our case manager, I noticed she was sweating, profusely. When I asked her if she was feeling alright, she said she had walking pneumonia. Why was she in school with this contagious illness? Walking pneumonia was the virus that Sierra was diagnosed as having reoccurring in her system which triggered the pans symptoms. Certain behaviors would be observed, such as OCD, fine motor depletion in handwriting, affecting the basal ganglia responsible for language, etc. This had been six to eight weeks into Sierra receiving stem cells. We quickly saw a decline in Sierra's behaviors with regards to focusing, attention, fine motor, speech, and other academic skills.

Sierra was another year older-seven years of age; a second chance. The first time, we were told Sierra had just shy of the amount that was considered normal in the stem cells working effectively, and making more of a difference, dependent on weight versus number of stem cells. We would give it a go.

Arriving Safely

We flew to Panama during a long plane ride stopping off in Dallas, Texas, and departing again to Panama City, Panama. Sierra was a wonderful little traveler.

We brought a couple of Peppa Pig coloring and sticker books, art supplies, etc.

We arrived on time, and what steamy hot weather! That was okay. We reached our destination. A gracious driver in a nice sedan picked us up all included from the Stem Cell Institute. It was about a half an hour car ride to the Hilton. It was evening, and fairly late, so we unpacked a little of our toiletries, took a quick shower and soon fell fast asleep. The next day we walked around, and went to a nice buffet that had breakfast included. Sierra loved the omelet station, and we were thrilled, as she hadn't eaten eggs for a little while now. There was lots of fruit, hot and cold cereals, pancakes, and bacon available. Sierra and I could eat the fruit, as it was gluten free. I ate an omelet, as well. Andy preferred hot cereal and granola. We went back to our rooms and decided to take a walk outside. Just as the doors opened, the wind got to us quickly and our umbrellas became inverted.

Perhaps, I would do a rain dance. I would perform any dance to see Sierra receive some more of the goods, as were in these stem cells. We decided to take a car service. After speaking to a nice young lad, who spoke both English and Spanish more proficiently and was a resident there, he helped us find a car that didn't eat a chunk of our money. We got into one of the taxis with noxious gases coming out of it. We were lucky, in our country. We went to the local grocery store to pick up some basics. Rice, quinoa, crackers, hummus, and guacamole.

That day, we had an appointment to come in and do a routine blood draw to see basic nutrition levels on vitamins, liver, and other organs. We went to a series of elevators that led us to the clinic which adjoined to our hotel. This was an added advantage to staying there.

As we reached one of the top floors where the clinic was, we had to use our card to get through the doorway where a lovely woman greeted us at the front desk. There were at least five other families there. Large open windows overlooking the city of Panama. We could see the river, tall buildings and the skies overhead. It was an almost panoramic view.

After a short while, we were welcomed to come through the doors and were greeted by the nurse. She took her vitals and then routine blood draw. Dr. Hernandez, our doctor, would come in soon. He approached us with a friendly smile, a warm demeanor. His voice was calm and reassuring. He answered any questions we had and offered support on whatever he could provide for us. He was attentive to Sierra, speaking with her in a kind and interested way. Just before we left, we asked about other families staying there that week. We were told there were twenty families that had children being treated. We left to go back to our rooms and got ready for the pool. We hoped to meet a few other families.

Greetings and Support

We chatted and got to know a couple of nice families there. There was one little boy who was five years of age. He was a real natural swimmer and a lover of the water. We'd wake up, peer out our large window, and see him bright and early in the morning. There really wasn't much to do there, however the families' presence and our connections in our individual struggles with our children's challenges made it a more welcoming place. We were supported in our quest for healing and to find more answers as the doctors performed their magic with the stem cells given.

Another family we met also had a little girl. She was about a year and a half younger than Sierra. Daphna was her name. What a sweet name, I thought. Daphna loved the I-Pad, and we noticed she was playing the video, Masha and Bear, which Sierra loved. It was just nice conversing about the simple things and having contact with others where communication was difficult, and they would understand how something small made their child's life a little brighter. Something to help them learn and grow and keep their mind's blossoming.

Sierra would circle around the pool dipping one foot in, then out. I imagined like Peppa Pig, the cartoon she loved, she jumped in the puddles there. She enjoyed kicking around the water and dabbling in the water at times. She went into the hot tub with a couple of little friends there said, "hi" and enjoyed for a while. Then, came out and dabbled her feet some more into the perimeter of the pool and at times, venture in just a little. It was cold and Sierra was not a fan of the temperature. She didn't mind the cooler air, but definitely not cold water. She loved the tub and the warmth of the heat upon her skin. Sometimes, I thought she didn't sense the temperature as much right away, but after a short while she had. It was a delay in sensory input, and that was something that we were addressing.

Toileting was a challenge. She wasn't feeling the sensation as quickly as it came. We hoped that this place had a peaceful and relaxing environment for Sierra to feel comfortable. Perhaps, that would help her regulate more throughout her days receiving treatment and afterwards. Even though we knew it was just a short while there, we heard of parents stating that their children said this or that or did this or that, even a day or two after receiving the cells. We didn't know if this was temporary or the circuitry being awakened in the system where the cells were screaming out, "Here I am. I'm coming to save the day." Boy, did we pray for this to happen.

Sierra continued to enjoy eating an omelet in the mornings. She loved the caramelized onions on the side. She would get seconds, even thirds, taking in around nine eggs at times. We started asking the man making them, if he wouldn't mind a double dose so we wouldn't have to return for another trip or two. He chuckled, seeming not to mind at all.

In the afternoon for lunch and later on during the evening for dinner, Sierra enjoyed ceviche, at the indoor/outdoor restaurant by the pool, salmon dishes and sushi with avocado. She had sushi and salmon at home, but we were thrilled about the ceviche, and the other white fish she was eating. One day, we went out for Indian food nearby. She loved the turmeric and cumin spices. She delighted in some of these dishes at home, too. Her palette seemed to be expanding some more. She was becoming more adventurous and willing to try.

Dr. Hernandez commented that Sierra could benefit from more omega's. Consuming fish helped, but he suggested giving her one tablespoon each day of omegas to be beneficial and to increase it, if she could stomach it. The results of the blood tests he administered seemed fine, overall. He encouraged more of the healthy fats, like butter and coconut oil, and probiotics for good healthy flora.

Our friend Rainie, Dafna's mom, shared with me that she noticed Sierra being more alert, focused, expressing more, and her increased overall affect. I noticed it, as well. I was pleased to have heard this from another's perspective.

After several days of being there, I woke up one morning to see something very different. I had to wipe my eyes a few times, as I saw that the bell's palsy on Andy's face had cleared up! Not entirely, but at least, fifty or sixty percent. I was quite amazed. As the days passed, I noticed it even more. Dafna had commented on it. So, had the doctor there. It was truly a miracle. It was a beneficial trip for my husband; For all of us.

We were soon to be leaving the hotel after being there for a week. We hadn't done much sightseeing as the doctors recommended to remain nearby to refrain from being in contact with any bugs, especially around the monkeys at the zoo. It could affect the stem cells, with viral components, etc. We did visit the Panama Canal. If you were there at the right time, you had the advantage of watching the ship going through it. It was low key, yet historical.

Off we went to the airport. We were asked to keep in touch with the doctors at certain times, several weeks, and then months. The institute emailed questionnaires at these intervals to chart how each child was progressing. Hopefully, they would come up with a method to help heal our children after tabulating all this information. We were grateful for their knowledge and hospitality there. We breathed in a sigh of relief, as it was followed by a smooth and easy flight. We were thrilled about returning home.

Taekwondo

When Sierra was about five years of age, we decided to try a sport she might find enjoyable. I heard about it from a friend of mine. We had gone to a birthday party where they had a taekwondo instructor held at an open play place. I searched for a technique that Sierra might enjoy rather than going to a sensory gym. I had grown frustrated at some of the techniques used when Sierra got upset, such as these oral vibrator tools. Sometimes, she got upset for other reasons, rather than needing sensory input. Perhaps, Sierra didn't want to do what another was asking her of because it was boring, or they were being too rote. Perhaps, they weren't playful enough for her liking. Maybe, she wasn't feeling well. It wasn't always that she needed pressure on her body or using a tool or instrument. Maybe, what she needed was a hug with reassurance and soft voice with, "Sierra it's okay", "I'm listening", "I'm here for you" or "We can do whatever you want, right now."

Here in our neighboring town, we found taekwondo. We went a year before, but Sierra wasn't feeling well enough the first two times we went. It was ten minutes away from where we resided. We drove into the large parking lot, where there was a superdome structure. A large gym was in the front. We walked down a large and long corridor. Leading to another large room, was a waiting room and adjacent to that, an even larger room with high ceilings, though slightly dark as there were no windows. It was filled with a bouncy house and a boat like flat swing, walking beams, a punching bag, and colored wooden like rods that fit into a vertical panel. Later, I found out it was to do kicks and to help with reasoning, problem solving, relationship building, decision making, organizing, etc.

Jordan was the taekwondo instructor. He came out with a white jacket and black belt wrapped around it, as appropriate for the sport. I watched how he gave Sierra just the right amount of space, moving forward, and back depending on her comfort level. He took her cues into consideration and he incorporated taekwondo postures. He encouraged Sierra to do "butterflies" with Sierra by sitting and flexing the knees outwards and up and down. Because it was taekwondo, some of it was structured and some wasn't. It took Sierra a few weeks before she gained a greater trust and an understanding of her body in space more to feel more at ease. In order to have integration occur, he understood that by teaching skills in a warm and inviting way, taking into great consideration the child's needs, so much could be learned in body, mind and spirit. Sierra's self-confidence and ability to integrate the movements, improved and expanded over time. Jordan utilized his knowledge from other areas and was always open to working with and capitalizing upon the child's innate potential. Sierra had built a trust in him. She was excited to see him, and would often bang on the door as soon as we got there, to dive right in. We saw changes in her ability to be calm and present and in using her mind and body to produce more integrated sounds in speech, as well.

One technique that Jordan used was in utilizing the rainbow-colored rods to coordinate, organize and synthesize connections in both the right and left hemispheres of the brain. Jordan asked, "Sierra kick the red, then, orange, yellow, green, blue, indigo, and then violet." (for left side of brain) Then, he'd ask, "Sierra, kick apple, tangerine, sunshine, grass, the sky, violet and cloud." (for right side of brain).

During the sessions, Jordan sometimes put her on his shoulders and spun her around, inviting some of those contagious belly laughs of her. Throughout the session, he offered her opportunities to walk across the beams, participate in somersaults on the mats, or go over to the bouncy house. It was a constructive and compassionate way of assisting Sierra. It offered her the opportunity to feel encouraged, giving her the space to develop trust and a commitment to moving at her pace. This allowed for the integration of skill development, as she acknowledged all aspects of her mind, body, and spirit.

I learned a greater understanding of taekwondo from a different perspective.

Jordan shared with me some interesting information about the brain and body. In taekwondo, they work from top to bottom and bottom to top, using one's arms and legs. With all those integral movements, "hiya's", and then, bowing as a completion, there was a beginning, middle, and end that aided in the cohesiveness of Sierra's development. All those kicks and side to side lateral movements, with the arms and legs being utilized in a cohesive way, her circuitry was making more connections.

A Blooming Artist

I continued to read to Sierra. Watching her face light up at some of her favorite books lit up my world. She continued to take them out, off of her shelves, and sometimes rip them when in a viral flare which seemed to be happening more, especially at certain times during the year. She put her hand to her mouth, then applied saliva. Sometimes, she poked holes in the faces of some of the characters. We continued to read together. I listened, slowed down and reminded myself when I got anxious or frustrated. I continued to go inwards and support her in using her own body. She enjoyed paints and pastels, markers and crayons, and I continued to encourage her and delight in her using them. Sometimes, I joined with her. Other times, I sat with her and give her space. I put music on softer children's music, classical, folk, and others. Sometimes, we moved our arms about and dance, before and after. We did some simple yoga poses, as well.

Sierra was a natural artist, great with color, combining and coordinating them, as seen when she got dressed. I placed her large easels out-one was a table easel and the other a stand-alone

one. She erroneously dipped her fingers in the paints and use the brushes, as well. She was immersed and focused for some longer periods of time, as she applied a variety of colors, typically in an abstract fashion on paper. At times, I offered her a canvas and supplied various options for her to use for textured effects. I had a variety of brushes and palette knifes. Often, she applied the edges to create different effects in the paints. Joyfully, she explored working with them. I was elated to see her making these large circles instead of the uniform and vertical lines from the linear type of program, Handwriting Without Tears. Here, the O.T. would start with making and modeling vertical lines typically in writing, and then move on to horizontal lines, then more curved and rounded shapes.

The repetitious movement of a dot to dot line formation and then moving onto the others, would cause greater OCD behaviors and restrictions in the brain. We are not static creatures, with only vertical lines around us. From the moment we are born, and we gain insight, we begin to see the colors, and the forms, and the shapes all around us. We take in the larger objects of the trees, with all sorts of dimensions from spherical roots to rectangular trunks, and circular inner, with outer elongated triangles for the leaves and squares within each. There are houses with all kinds of patterns within them. We need to depend on this natural distinction born from a human perspective, and not from a more technological one from the computer screen. We are multi-dimensional beings and it is essential, as part of our growth process to use all elements within us, as contained in our bodies, to become more integrated human beings.

Emerging Speech

Jerri was Sierra's most current speech therapist. We started about nine months ago. Sierra had been seven years old. When I first spoke with Jerri, I immediately was taken by her compassion and willingness to meet children where they were at. There were just too many instances where I saw others working in a teacher directed way, without taking into consideration children's feelings, from an intuitive standpoint.

I was reminded of a speech therapist we had seen a couple of months prior, that immediately brought her over to the corner of her office space, as she pulled out a tiny table in a chair, just inches from the wall. She sat opposite her while delegating commands to her. Never again, I thought. How was this engaging her, especially having global apraxia.

Jerri spoke from the heart. She shared how much she truly was interested in what Sierra's interests were and welcoming us in the sessions. She embraced parent's feedback and continued that it was essential to understand Sierra from a more intimate and broader perspective. She had a large space with a couple of different rooms.

One room had a swing, a small slide, and large oversized ball to bounce on. Jerri followed Sierra's lead and interjected when she saw it was necessary.

As the next few sessions passed, Sierra developed a nice rapport with Jerri. She was happy to go and gave her a hug. Jerri had an appreciation for art and music and would integrate the two into the sessions. She was highly trained in the PROMPT method, as well as others, for essential cueing, to aide Sierra's approximations and articulations of sounds in words.

Staying present was critical for Sierra and providing her with choices of interest. Joanne agreed, wholeheartedly. Early on, one day I came in to participate in a session, and during it she commented, "Wow, Sierra says so much more having you here". I was thrilled she saw that by slowing down and in the subtleties of each incremental movement, there was an interaction not always visibly, seen. It was held within the intricacies in the tenderness of each moment. There were words that would sometimes come to the surface, having greater expression. Calming and engaging the mind and body, building upon trust, as in the engagement of two people, was key.

A Moment

I reflected back to those hard and trying times. I sat in my bed peering out the window. It was a cold wintry day, and the branches stood naked. They were not hidden behind foliage. They were interdependent upon each another. The sun shined upon them, enriching the soils. Cascading water had dripped down from its branches from the previous snowfall. Their rootedness allowed them to stand firm in the storms that they weathered. They had mercy on one another by establishing their own independence.

My quest was to forgive and let go. To breathe in goodness. Where was the separation of our lives? We were the same, we were different. I was her mother. She was my child. I loved her so.

A Letter to Mine Self:

It was December 29. 2017. I had been writing to myself more frequently. Essential that I opened up something, this gift long held within me. I dabbled in at times to write something sentimental to myself. I honed in.

A Gift:

Seek, but not the answers.
Go within the body.
Where lies the pain?
Is it within the heart?
If it is within the heart,
Ask it, "What do you need?"
"Love."
Where does it begin and what happened in the middle?
Did something from your past cause any suffering?
If you go deeper, the answers will reveal themselves.

There I was—
I sat in my Big Wheels car.
I was six years of age.
I'm wearing pig tails.
I'm smiling—this knowing smile.
I could see the wisdom in my eyes, an old soul, and yet, a sadness.
Something was hidden.
I was alone.
Trust versus distrust.
I had to let go-
My loneliness was in part caused by internalizing my parent's pain.
Fears…
I could not be enough, if I was always holding onto something my
    mom wouldn't or couldn't allow within herself to accept or be.
I needed to break through these chains.
Within this process, I reclaimed a greater love.
I was not to absorb anyone else's pain.

I was responsible for the breadth, depth, and beauty of my soul's
   development.
To love myself, unconditionally.
My daughter's wings would not be clipped.
She would fly amongst the clouds.
She would soar in the sky.
I would fly alongside her.
She would find her way.

Waste Not,
Want Not

I gave complements because it felt good, not for approval. I was honest and open to my child, letting her know she was doing a great job with even the smallest acts of scribbling a picture. I was inclined to not over-do it or do it for her.

Unconditionally speaking, I wanted so much for Sierra, for her to thrive.

I realized that I could not give her more than she was capable of receiving.

That was enough.

She was deserving of so much in life,

I wished for her the simple things;

To use her hands to write her name.

To use her voice to say no, with greater ease.

To speak more naturally.

To be able to integrate whatever she needed to for purposes of using the bathroom, etc.

To independently get herself dressed, as well as put on her socks and shoes.

To place her jacket in the appropriate arms, attach the zipper in the grooves, and zip up.

To become more independent, share her wants, needs, thoughts and feelings, more naturally.

This was not something unusual.

It was something any parent would want for their child.

This was something I dreamed about and wished for.

It was something bearing a typical development.

Many parents didn't have to think about this.

The questions were similar,

Did you do your homework?

Is it done properly?

Did you practice your dance routine?

It was simple conversation.

I needed to breathe in the good in life and exhale the unhealthy things that I was holding onto.

To rise above*

I prayed for greater support and for optimal healing on all levels.

To walk out of our house without worry that Sierra would have an accident, or if Sierra screamed, or perhaps left my side or ran somewhere.

I wanted for her to feel comfortable and at peace, regardless of the reactions of others, from ignorance or fear.

This was our normal. I hadn't wanted to waste another moment sinking into something out of fear or desperation. It was essential that I acknowledged this perfectly, beautiful day.

Our rhythm of life was imperfectly, perfect.
It was essential that I slowed down when my heart was racing.
There was nothing to catch up to.

It was essential to step up to the plate, and as I did, to acknowledge
the plate I was on. It was okay. Second base would come when
we kept our eye on the ball.
To never back down from the fly ball.
It was coming towards us, not at us.
It was a gift, in itself.
This was the present, our lives.
Today.

To forgive myself.
Balance was key.
Three bases, like the bases of three, symbolizing the great masters
in astrology.
The fourth, led us home and represented the angels, as in the
number four.
The masters and the angels led us home.
A home run was found.
An epiphany.
Yes. Exactly, at this moment.
To appreciate, such as this!

Collages

I had been creating collages with Sierra, even more so when she started ripping at her books. Sometimes, she would poke at pictures within it. This occurred during these more cyclical times having pans, and autoimmune issues surfacing. I even wrote a story called, "Pieces" to share more about having compassion for another whose OCD ran wild.

How could I help her fit the pieces of her life together? When all of this was happening in her mind and body, I focused on spirit, and allowed the creativity to flow and to manifest. When I grew impatient and worried, when nothing else seemed to suffice—painting did, art did.

Sierra enjoyed art activities. We often took out scissors, water-color paints, and pencils, and large heavy white paper. I assisted Sierra in cutting, assisting her at times, I moved my wrists as well to show more angularity allowing for more fluidity. Sierra turned over the pieces to adhere to the glue she squeezed out with all her strength, but at times, needed a little support in. That was an area where she had hypotonia in, just above her wrist. Also, we had performed wheel barrows and crab crawling in physical therapy, and at home. We had a large tube she crawled through. I placed objects inside of it and ask her what she found as she neared the end.

By using one's whole body making large rounded brush strokes in up and down movements, and more circular forms from a less restrained and more fluid approach, I hoped Sierra would release restrictions held within her body.

School seemed to focus on more simplified forms of artwork. Perhaps, because her teacher didn't have an art room, and so she came into the classrooms, so she had art a la carte. It was more difficult to do more elaborate activities. Still, some variation of media would have been more stimulating for stirring the imagination. Sierra came home with a lot of tissue paper collages. The tissue paper was carefully glued with each piece being practically, the same size, and placed, so uniformly, onto a piece of paper. Children would learn about various artists. However, it was so much of the same type of media. It would have been helpful to see the usage of other types of media including cardboard, natural sticks or twigs, textured paper, overlaying of colors with different media, and objects for different effects.

Life was not about doing the same thing, day in and day out, without some zing in it. Wearing the same outfit laid out for us every day or eating the same meal could prove to be mundane. Life was a collage. It was more than a static flow. There was so much meaning gained upon exploring materials and concepts.

Instilling courage by smiling, laughing, engaging, all the while enjoying the simplicity of being together was important. The cutting, and pasting, tearing, and applying and painting—all of it was to be delved into, to experiment with. Who knew where it would take us! The unknown.

People First

Throughout my days, I spent countless hours writing to both our home district's school and the school she was attending. It could have been anything from how Sierra's week was or requesting more support for services, etc. Transportation was a key issue. I had been driving Sierra to school, since November that past year. The lovely women who were transporting her for the past two months from September until November, were hired as an emergency after the other drivers didn't work out. I thought they could transport her until at least, the end of the year. However, they were taken off the route. Her driver, Talia, shared with my husband and I on a Monday morning, that Thursday would be their last day. Thankfully, my husband happened to be at home that day. My heart sank. I gasped. I couldn't believe it. Maybe, there was a way to have them continue driving Sierra. I knew it wouldn't be easy. Still, I had hope. These women sang to her, asked about her interests, and laughed with her. As we walked outside in the morning at pick up, I heard, "Good morning, Siiii eeerrrra." Enthusiastically, the driver always made Sierra feel at home having a sense of humor and compassion. Nellie the aide, was warm and gentle towards Sierra. That day Andy, Sierra and I went to the Board of Education in our town. We walked up to the front desk where the secretary welcomed us. We gave her a brief run down as to why we showed up. She said, "Oh, you want to speak with Dr. Rivera, the Head of Business Administration.

We waited for a short time, though in anticipation, it seemed much longer. Finally, Dr. Rivera came out. He had a kind demeanor. We were led into his office and shared what happened. Within that time, he reassured us that the new company had a wonderful reputation and that we would be happy with them. I emphasized that it was really important to us, that Sierra continued with the drivers on this route. Dr. Rivera shared, he would be in touch with us, after speaking with Leslie, the Region 1 Administrator for transportation. He also mentioned that if I wanted to drive our daughter, I would be compensated. I shared it was a far drive, and like city driving. In the morning it could take forty-five to fifty minutes to get there. He nodded as if he understood. Then, proceeded to get up. He would be in touch with us in the next day or so.

That night we decided to go to Home Depot to get a Hanukkah/Christmas Tree for Sierra, and our family. We got a small tree whose lights were generated by solar heat. We had panels on our house, so we figured what better tree to celebrate the holiday. Even though the light in our eyes dimmed that day, I reminded myself of the true meaning of the holiday season. There were more miracles for us, all to be received.

I called Willamina, the owner of Bright Transportation. She said she'd give a call over to Leslie and find out what she could do. We went home that day in anticipation of what would happen next. We awaited their call. I was motivated to find out as much as I could to move forward. Kind, loving, supportive people in Sierra's life meant so much to us. Something as simple as a bus ride became a blessing. These ladies were Sierra's friends. They were our friends, too.

The Next Days

I decided to write to Ms. Farida, the assistant to the special education director, and our case manager. I kept in contact with Willamina. I asked her if she could share with me anything in the contract that would provide a greater understanding for me, from a legal standpoint. It read that when the threshold was met, bidding would occur. Andy contacted the State Education Department. The contents that contained what the threshold meant, was disclosed to Andrew. It was also shared with me by Dr. Rodriquez, disclosing the amount of being around seventeen thousand dollars. The state reported its threshold at nineteen thousand dollars. They were being paid two hundred and forty-five dollars a day, approximately. I didn't understand this, as it was two months, and the bidding was not up, yet. Surely, nineteen-thousand would not have been utilized until sometime in the month of March.

When I reached out to Leslie, she informed me that bidding occurred three times a year. November, which had just ended, as we were in the month of December, and March and then, May/June. She shared that the threshold would have been up before

March, so she rebid it out. There was no ethical or moral reasoning to this. I contacted the mayor and our local congress person. Also, I reached out to a close friend of mine to inquire about her friend, a newscaster for a television network. She welcomed any stories from us that consisted of enough valid information that she could assist with. She continued that it could be from an ethical, moral standpoint, as well as legal. I emailed her information and spoke with her on the phone. She would present it to the I-Team and see what she could do. However, I hadn't enough documentation to prove a legitimate enough case.

It was two days prior to having the new transportation company arrive. Still, I hadn't known their name. I contacted my case manager. She was lovely and new this year, with some prior experience. She emailed be back the name of the company. Also, I contacted Leslie who informed me of their name. I decided to look them up on the web, yet could not locate a source, anywhere. I called Leslie, a second time. Graciously, she provided me with their number. Having concerns, I called and asked if they would back out of the contract to help support our daughter and family. The woman who answered, shared she would have the owner contact me. He returned my call. After speaking a short while, I asked him if Leslie ever contacted him to ask if he could begin in three weeks, instead of right away. The winter break was approaching. We would be able to give Sierra some time to acclimate, rather than starting the day after, she awaited her friends to come. The owner said that Leslie never called to ask them start in January. He also disclosed to me that he was twenty-one years old, and that he had been in business since, that past March. They were eight months old and had not held a track record.

I sat down with Sierra, letting her know I would be driving her that upcoming Friday. It turned out that she didn't feel well. Thankfully, we had the weekend to prepare our daughter to explain to her that our friends were not continuing with the drive. I shared with her that it wasn't her fault, and that they were asked to do another route.

Still, the drivers of the company parked in front of our house every day. Kindly, I asked them to park down the road to avoid any emotional upset. I was unable to cancel the route, unless I signed a waiver for transportation services as mandated in her IEP for the year. I was not prepared to do that. I called a meeting with the case manager, and the team, with hope that this could be resolved.

Status Quo

I suppose the meeting went well. Voices weren't raised. I remained open-minded and expressed my thoughts in as thorough and articulate manner, as I could. I wanted to believe that they regarded Sierra to be more than just a number, and that she'd be valued. They couldn't put in the contract that Sierra needed an English-speaking aide. They could put, "Preferably speaks English." This was nonsense. It was what Willamina, the owner from Bright Transportation called, "Reverse Discrimination". That was definitely, what this was. I understood about immigration and being respected and culturally diversity being welcomed. I was a proponent of that.

However, "What about having special needs and children that had communication disorders?!" "What about Us?" Pink's song came to mind. What about fairness and moral standards? If a child has a communication disorder, I would assume that would take precedence over the language that an aide was fluent in. This was more than an ethical issue. The law was not always so clear cut and defined. For fairness and with equality, I fought for my daughter. Year after year, I came out with a fierceness. I had an undying passion for the rights of my daughter.

No one in that room and outside our kitchen walls was standing up for us, for our little girl, for our family. I hadn't known why this would surprise me anymore, then it already had during these past seven years. These were the first seven years of our daughter's life. The only life she knew.

I pictured myself in a boxing match putting up my duke's. There were many parents in our town who hired both advocates and lawyers when they wanted something of importance from the district. Was this survival of the fittest? What was the principal of defining what our children truly needed? It was essential to have integrity to provide what was morally and ethically sound.

The Right Place

We moved to a pretty town with a variety of restaurants and cafes. Maggie enjoyed her daily walks with her dog friends. Sometimes, Sierra enjoyed the walks after school with her. Even though Maggie, was ten years of age, still she was sprite, a high jumper, and expressive. We sang as we walked down the street. Sierra used the curb like a balance beam. We galloped together and run with Maggie. Maggie gave me a tug here and there, pulling me further. Sierra did, too.

Once in a while, we saw someone outside or arriving back home. It seemed like everyone was always in a hurry to get somewhere. I knew that children, most likely had after school activities, or academia support. There was one little boy, Randy, who was a couple of years younger. He was sweet, polite, and attentive to Sierra. He wanted to play with her. It was refreshing. It warmed my heart to see them play chase. I invited their family over a few times to play on the trampoline. Yet, we barely saw them or anyone outside. I hoped that one day they would come around and knock on our door.

When you have a communication challenge, whether people expressed it or not, they avoided situations, or appeared disinterested. In addition, the media was not addressing what most special needs parents were experiencing. There was a show on television called, "The Good Doctor". This was about a young man with Asperger's Disorder, who had a genius-like intelligence. What about the children and adults who experienced greater struggles? Would they ever be "enough" to be accepted in our society, or did they have to become a good doctor, or pursue another prestigious profession to be valued, seen and heard? Would they ever have the opportunity to go to college? It is beneficial for others to see what many families' lives are like on an everyday basis. We, as a society need not to hide what is seen as too large an imperfection. This is our future.

The autistic girl created on Sesame Street. She was adorable. Did she have potty training issues, meltdowns, communication challenges, fine and gross motor challenges? Perhaps, she did. However, it was a cartoon. Yes. It was helpful for children. Adults need to accept what is happening in our world. This is a growing epidemic that needs to be addressed.

We continued our quest to support our daughter with proper care and treatment. We had an appointment coming up in two weeks. It was with an immunologist. Perhaps, she would provide us with more answers.

The Immunologist

Our hour-long drive trip to the hospital was quite uneventful, in terms of our conversation. Andy and I were both tired. My husband's phone short circuited, and he was invested in getting it to work so that we could see the route. A dark blank screen appeared on his navigating device. He decided to accept the use of my phone and quickly assembled it on the dash board. Andy loved his devices, as he was a high technology kind of guy. We had Alexa at home which I enjoyed in part, and all the right cords to charge up all our electronics. Me, I was sensitive to excess stimuli, and it concerned me for Sierra's well-being.

I felt a separation between us in the car ride there. I tried to reacclimate myself and calm my thoughts by listening to music. Andy and I were not on the same page when it pertained to having more concrete evidence on a subject matter. I relied on my intuition, and ideas, as well as research. Andy was much more literal than me and needed to see facts about the validity in a statistical way. He had a lighter side to him, with an appreciation for down time. We both were missing more of that.

We were both tired and needed some relaxation. In our daily routines, just sitting for a while was surely a break. A vacation sounded lovely. That was on my bucket list. We arrived at the hospital. Andy hadn't worn a jacket on in the cold wintry weather. The wrinkles from his forehead were apparent, and his attire was representative of his state of being. He wore a mauve, somewhat faded sweatshirt that was half tucked in. He was overdoing it with things that needed to get done. I admired the dedication he had to help our family, at work, and without a doubt, spending most of his time with Sierra.

We were in the waiting room. I went up to the secretary and gave her our credit card and insurance information. Before I could even sit down, Andy asked me how long the wait would be. He was on fast dial, calculating the next steps. More so than normal. He was edgy. I had given the woman our insurance information. His response was, "Oh, you were there for a while, so I just assumed. I got up to ask her and when I returned a nurse called, "Sierra Schwartz". I took in a huge breath and tried to let go of any pressures to relax for the moment. Perhaps, we'd have more answers.

We were led down a short corridor. It was typical of a doctor's office in a hospital setting, sterile with minimal décor. Dr. B. introduced herself and was welcoming. She commented that she read Dr. M.'s analysis of Sierra. Dr. M., a neurologist we saw who tested Sierra for pans/pandas and shared she had symptomologies of this disorder and had recommended her. Since Sierra's histamine levels were really high, he thought, perhaps an immunologist could help. She said she'd check her white blood cell count and other areas involved with the immune system. She spoke a little low and the dialect and pronunciation of words were a little hard to understand, as she had somewhat of an accent. She was of Japanese descent. This was pertinent information and I listened intently, to be sure I understood most of it. I had an appreciation of other languages and cultures. Being somewhat skilled in my decoding of sounds, I was able to decipher much of the information.

She believed that Sierra could have ADD and OCD and yeast, but wasn't certain of the pans, after briefly reading the blood tests Dr. M. had sent to us. I hadn't understood her reasons for this. There were so many viruses a person could contract, and we couldn't possibly test for all of them. Dr. B. asked about our history and Sierra's overall birth process. After about an hour of speaking with her, she believed that Sierra's challenges were auto-immune induced from vaccinations. She wasn't certain if in fact, anything was related to a genetic disposition to having a language challenge, such as apraxia prior to birth. My husband had severe dyslexia. Apraxia was from similar region of the brain. Still, any smaller challenges developed and multiplied, as a cascading effect after receiving vaccines.

Dr. B. stated that she wanted to put us in a study for auto-immune induced autism. She needed more information from bloodwork. She took out tubes and a needle. I asked her if there was a lab in the hospital. Dr. B. shared since this was part of her study, she needed to perform this outside of a lab. Sierra sat on Andy's lap, as he helped with steadying her arm. She turned to me. I tried to console her, maintaining my composure, while rubbing her back. I noticed the doctor was a bit shaky and wasn't able to retrieve enough blood from her right arm. It seemed like a long while to find a vein. In addition, I was not comfortable with needles and the sight of blood made me queasy.

I requested the doctor to kindly, remove it and try obtaining it from the other arm. Respectfully, she removed the tube with the needle from her arm. We tried again. Deep breath in, I told myself, as she placed that little butterfly in her left arm. Immediately, the blood flowed through, however it stopped shortly after. When I looked down, I noticed a knot in the cord. The blood couldn't make it through. She asked me to hold it and assist her with this. I was mortified. Sierra was getting more agitated. She looked down at her arm, as she typically did while having blood drawn. I asked the doctor to please take it out. I asked how much was in the vile. She shared it was about sixty percent, and that she'd get as much information as she could. If we chose to complete the rest of the tests needed to determine more, such as allergies at a local laboratory, we'd would do so at another time. Then, she postured towards my husband and in a wispy voice and low tone said, "Mom should stay out." I replied, "Excuse me, in an understated yet, inquisitive tone." "The cord was in a knot." She said that Sierra somehow got the cord in a knot. I wasn't sure how that could be. An honest mistake however, to blame Sierra was not taking responsibility for her actions. We thanked for her time and proceeded to leave.

I was disappointed that Andy didn't speak up more. While I understood being uncomfortable in situations like these, it was important that he shared his feelings more. "Marni, I know this is hard. We'll figure the next step out and do it together." Instead, it was silence.

Prior to leaving, we had to fill out the information on the forms for the study the doctor was conducting. When I read a question about nighttime ritual activities, I had difficulty with this, and wasn't very focused on it. I handed over the form to Andy and asked if he could fill out the rest. He had to circle an item, one through five, on a continuum. I took Sierra to the bathroom. She was crying and screaming. When we entered, she grew calmer. Just as we opened the door to turn to the waiting area, Andy got up and handed the form to the secretary. As we walked briskly to the car, I felt drained. Just as I got into the seat and buckled myself in, my dear friend Tara's name appeared on my cell phone. I was hesitant to pick up, as I knew it would be a difficult time to communicate with her. She could tell from my tone and reluctance in sharing more, that it wasn't good timing. I spoke in quick responses, in sort of code. She tried to summarize my thoughts, and supported me, with caring and consoling words. She was a dear friend, a soul sister.

A New Day

The sun rose. I woke up. I rubbed my eyes, as I looked out the window. Frost was forming on the branches of an old tree. I breathed in and exhaled out reminding myself that I had something to live for. My beautiful girl was here on this earth. This compelled me to get up and face the day.

I stretched my tired limbs out of bed, helped Sierra wash up, get dressed, and brush her hair. Then downstairs we went, sometimes with a song. When we got to the bottom, we would often, look in the mirror and making silly faces. Next, I made her breakfast and gathered up her lunch. It was typically, half prepared from the prior evening. I segued to the corner cabinet to get Maggie's dog food, then towards the sink to fill her bowl with water. Then, I zig zagged back to make that cup o' fresh organic mountain grown coffee, to be poured into my favorite bright yellow mug. It had "Cup o' Sunshine" on it. A little bit o' sunshine, a reminder for me of what existed inside of me. That kick of caffeine to start my day, worked wonders.

At around 7:00 am, after I had her lunch and snack bag packed, I might take a look at her speech book if I hadn't the night prior. Her notes were very thorough and organized, with a few notes on it. I responded, typically with a sentence or two in the small space next to it and sign my initials. I would clean out the dish washer or do some quick folding of laundry. I preferred doing it in the morning. I gathered items up from the tables and the floor, such as books, papers, or toys.

I drove Sierra in my sturdy super-duper Subaru to school. It was great in the snow, having four-wheel drive. It was comforting to me to take her there. It wasn't the fact that I received three thousand plus dollars, at thirty dollars a day, from January until the rest of the school year. Sierra would be in safe hands and treated well. We chatted and sand and played music on the way there. Snacks were readily available.

I was being a mom. I was not the most organized, however I tried to create a place that was optimal for Sierra to thrive in. I thought about the team effort. Our home district recommended all ABA programs which were specifically for autism, not apraxia. Sierra was social, having good receptive abilities. She had a great personality, and a sense of humor. She didn't fit a typical mold. She needed an approach with more emphasis on utilizing her body to produce speech in a slow and steady way, with greater attention to affect, pitch and tone with expressive communication and within a social-emotional context.

Again, I prefaced Sierra being a global learner with the apraxia component being her largest challenge. I continued to place emphasis on this and search for more of a language-based program, as it was better suited for her needs. I researched heavily.

I followed up in an email restating how a communication-based program, with language serving as the key element was essential for Sierra's individual needs. Sierra had an IEP, an Individualized Educational Program. I was determined to find a school that could and would modify a program. This was least restrictive for Sierra's needs. We asked for a program that wasn't miles away, unless it was one that suited her needs for communication challenges. I awaited their response. There was one school we were interested in for children with learning challenges. We remained optimistic.

A Greater Hope

Yes! Today was the day. I noticed Sierra was verbally expressing more. And not simply, the word "more" which was expostulated on, in almost every meeting as thee context word that Sierra had expressed. This was along with, her having used the symbol for more. It felt like Ground Hogs Day.

Today: Today I heard from Sierra's teacher in an email, "Sierra is communicating a lot in school". It delighted me any time I heard positive statements about Sierra's progress. For Sierra to communicate more, to state her truths, to speak her mind, and her heart. To feel comfortable and safe, and to feel well. My brave girl, forge ahead. I knew it was coming, although there were all these passages of time and variability, due to her suppressed immune system. Her great tenacity, her inner spirit, and joyfulness would always, serve her well. Sierra was here to teach us something BIG. Our little girl was using her VOICE, more and more.

I knew at the ripe age of seven years old, there was so much that could happen inside of Sierra. Sierra had a spark inside of her. We continued to work diligently with support from those who believed in her. We were grateful to family members, the small family we had, for close friends to be there in whatever way they could. This day would forever hold true. "Sierra is communicating a LOT at school." At home she was, too. I was inspired to continue reading to her. I was driven to continuously support her overall health. A healthy track of life.

Communicating further, I had a recent phone conversation with her teacher.

As a parent this meant so much. She cared about Sierra and welcomed us in anytime. Being able to share more about Sierra, to help her understand her greater, and to work together as a team was so helpful.

Waking up in the morning was easier knowing we were a part of a team who cared. I continued to focus on what Sierra truly enjoyed. She loved books with puppies and dogs in them. One was called, "Lady Bug Girl". Another was called, "Snuggle Puppy of Mine.", and she appreciated other books with animals in them. She'd participate in reading them, adding in words, and I'd go slower. Books with rhythm and song she loved, as music was part of her great passion. We spent a good portion of our days dancing together. Also, she had a piano she dabbled in. I played for her some well-known songs, others I made up. I was finding my own rhythm throughout all of this. With acceptance of our squiggly selves, we would emerge into a more harmonious rhythm with ourselves, and one another. An outside of the lines approach to learning was the key to our individualities.

Aligning with Ourselves

Out of the box thinkers, feelers, lovers, and dreamers. Sierra and I continued to be creative. We used various sized brushes and got our hands wet with finger painting. Art was not to be defined by solely, small movements, but large gross motor movements. The freedom to build upon inductively was essential for us, instead of a deductive model of thinking. My goal was to work on developing greater perspective, and not in small parameters. The strategy of shrinking oneself into a box was not going to be of benefit. Labels were not essential for self-discovery in our uniqueness, as individuals. The proof of the pudding was in the process of it, and the fun and interaction of making it. Even better was one that wasn't already contained or premade from a box.

Mother earth was right outside our doorstep. We often visited a local farm and ate from the rich minerals of the land. It was given freely, naturally, not consumed by industry standards, and excess fillers and toxic chemicals. Finding a naturalistic pediatrician wasn't going to happen, if there weren't any in our area and with weekend hours. There was that voice in my ear saying, "Marni- You have to find someone, trust someone, a doctor, a therapist, a person that could help Sierra more."

With a gulp in my throat, I reminded myself, I was doing all I could. I was also that someone that was part of helping Sierra grow the most. Others were doing their best, I suppose, even though it didn't always feel like it. People didn't always have the answers. Either the interest or the understanding wasn't there. Perhaps, it was sheer ignorance. Also, some might rather hide their head in a plume of smoke, then face reality. I had little choice. I had to go easier on myself. Life was a road map. Sometimes, signs were hidden in a lot of hills and valleys. I reminded myself, "I was here for the ride."

My Thank You Letter
(Perhaps, one day you will read.
You will always understand.)

Dear Sierra,

There will come a time where you will come to see, that all is exactly where it's meant to be. Perhaps, you already do. You understand something deeper, beyond what's the ideal, as you use your senses to navigate through life. It is your love of learning, sharing with others, and being exactly who you are. Your inner beauty shines. When you are in the comforts of others, it is here that you find greater purpose, and an inner peace undefined. Your reflection, in your capacity to share your wisdom and your grace becomes clearer.

I have always known your gift, to see beyond. At a very young age of one and a half, you showed me your feelings and thoughts in pictures from books, from stories and images that sparked an interest and a way to express your innermost thoughts. I knew that you were intuitive, bright and very determined. You had charisma, you understood emotions on such a deep level. You will read to others and become their teachers. You will share your story.

This is my gift to you, dear love. May you find your inner peace, inner strength, in all your glory to heal those places inflicted upon you. It was not because you deserved this, but because of a streak of something you could not accept, and rightly so, in your little body...

In your mind's eye and in your heart that was golden, I knew you would come out of this and into your own. You, Sierra, are a mentor, a guide, a creative thinker, and an inventive soul. You will speak a thousand words or however long a string of thoughts in your unique way.

You will share your story. Believe in YOU. Sierra Brooke. From the very beginning... You were determined to stay in my cocoon, so comfortable you were.

I saw your soulful eyes, as I closed mine, just prior to your birth. They eluded a brightness so effervescent. You knew me, and I knew you. You felt me, and I felt you. Then you came, and here you are. With great wisdom and inner strength, in the here and now, lies the present. The gift of YOU!

Jagged edge of a mountain; Merge into the stream of life. You were destined for this.

The words become alive in whatever form they arrive. You have manifested your glory, and have achieved your dream. You are forever, loved.

The Day After—
Pans and More

A letter from school: "Sierra was having a rough morning, bouts of crying and screaming. However, it didn't last long." Another letter that day shared that Sierra tried to take her shirt off before lunch followed by, "I had never seen her do that before."

Welcome to the wonderful world of pans/pandas. A place where there were riptides of effects, such as wiping saliva on books, ripping small lines in increments on pages on books, sucking on pieces of paper, biting nails, etc. I was trying to control some of these overly anxious behaviors with supplements and herbs. I gave Sierra goldenseal, and vitamin C, vitamin D, oregano oil, at intervals, turmeric, and garlic. It was an endless battle to uncover and discover what would indeed work. We tried a regular course of antibiotics, but Sierra didn't seem any better and wasn't able to tolerate another one. She spit it up at times, or refused it. Natural supplements were preferred anyway. Alternating goldenseal and oregano seemed to help. It wasn't always so cut and dry. We altered dosages and diet. She was gluten free, but sometimes had dairy.

She ate fairly well for a child, but during a flare up, she might not eat much at all or crave certain things like pickles, and chocolate. Pickles had a lot of vinegar which was acidic, so I didn't give her these much. Dark chocolate had anti-oxidants in it, which wasn't so bad, it was more of the sugar that was an issue. Obviously, sleep was important. Added pressure or stress could bring out symptoms, as well as coming in contact with the actual viruses.

I researched more. We needed a team of doctors, teachers, and therapists to work together. However, everything was piecemealed. Little community, and schools were at a distance. It was difficult, all of it. If we could truly identify what was occurring, giving her the beneficial nutrients, and remove the impurities with the right techniques, we could continue to heal.

Sierra had a methylation issue. We received tests results back from a holistic medical doctor. It revealed she had two homozygous genes called, A1298C and C677T, a rare and more severe kind of a genetic mutation of MTHFR. The MTHFR gene processes amino acids, the building blocks of protein. Her body was not designed to absorb the components in the vaccines. It was a NO for any VACCINES for her.

I continued to look at our diet, our food supply, and our water system, etc. A maps doctor; I became my own. I would never stop. Sierra continued to remind me, in her endless courage, to never give up.

I couldn't keep Sierra in a bubble. I had been sick for the past couple of days. No fever, but a sore throat and lethargic, so she could have caught a virus from me. I tried not to breathe on her. It was hard because Sierra was so affectionate and wanted to snuggle with me. I would rub her back, and feet, caress her head and kiss her on her crown.

The What If's

That people pleasing attitude came through me as my heart pulsed faster. "I'm good enough". "You're good enough". I had been uncovering more, accepting more, and not internalizing things. We all had our own ways of coping. I was learning and growing at my own rate. I couldn't be on fast gear in this flight or fight mode. I could only, do so much at one time. I couldn't prevent Sierra from having flare ups. I couldn't keep her in a bubble away from germs and from exploring. I had to focus on the now, to not be afraid of what tomorrow would bring.

I recalled a dream. I held a red bag in my hand with the word fear on it. I dumped it out. I was at an airport standing in between two corridors. One was to my left, and the other to the right. Which way? I questioned. The right way. Leave the past behind.

All the what ifs? I had enough of the what ifs. It fed into fear. If others chose to act harshly with judgment or criticism, that was their choice. I was responsible for my own actions and reactions. I couldn't change others. I could respond in a way that was more favorable for my highest good. Even when buttons were pushed,

I could take a step back, reflect on what I was feeling, and ask myself, what purpose this situation served. If I couldn't do it in the moment, I needed to honor myself, by removing myself, speak my piece if I chose in an honorable way, and move on. Situations would show up at exactly the right time, testing me. Patience, my dear. Patience, I reminded myself. It was never too late.

Any unruly reactions from others, the gaped mouths, the widened eyes filled with disparity, with underlying issues of remorse or shame, or whatever it was that others were experiencing when my daughter's voice became escalated, was theirs to acknowledge, or not to. If Sierra cried or screamed, it was okay. This too, shall pass.

Maybe, maybe not. It is what it is. Breathe.

It was essential to live, learn, and let it be. Lift up the heart, that is the "if", the condition served, like the reasoning to look deeper. Like a face lift—that was where the smiley faces existed. Love life for what it is. "Let it Be". With appreciation for John Lennon; I heard his song playing in my head from time to time. The first stanza, "When I find myself in times of trouble, Mother Mary comes to me. Speaking words of wisdom, let it be."

Motherhood for me; It wasn't planned in any mommy-manual. I did my best. I slipped, at times. I needed to remind myself, "It's okay to fall. I could pick myself up. If Sierra fell to the floor in a tantrum, it was alright. A message to slow down, to simply be. I could shrug my shoulders with a "So what?" "So, she almost took her shirt off." "So, she screamed!" "So, she cried!" Sierra was communicating. This was her symphony. This was her voice. Today.

I had a choice. I could laugh. I could cry. I could be angry. I could feel whatever it was that arose. This was a part of our daily lives. There were smiles. There were tears. There were moments when all else stopped where nothing else mattered. We had the ability to pick ourselves up. Our perceptions could change as we gained greater clarity, and we understood and appreciated something even more powerful within us;

The little things. The ones that mattered so much. The one's that remind us of hope, of resilience, and of joy. Through it all, I watched my little girl, in admiration of her. She had the power, the ability, the knowledge, and the passion. She was as wise as her great grandmother.

This was life. It was our lives. This world was becoming inundated with more children with compromises. By accepting the greater wisdom in us all, with humility, respect, and with compassion, we could all serve as guiding force to aid in a piece to an unforgiving puzzle that was created. Children with these challenges, are more than the pieces within a puzzle. They are whole. We each have our own maps inside of us, that are unique. In our journeys, we are our greatest sources of strength. Within our innate potential, we will find the answers. Coming together in a team effort is the most harmonious way, for our voice to be heard.

More Days After

There were days I was compelled to sit down and feverishly write my story. To get the message out, to set the record straight. I could remember those much simpler times in the seventies and eighties. Those turn style record players. It took a little time to motor plan, to put the record on it, and place the needle, ever so accurately on the song. The scratches on it left an imprint, offering a greater appreciation for me, to tend to it, more carefully. We couldn't just press a button to put on our favorite song or show or latest video game. It required time and patience.

I reminded myself of the goodness within. I regained the fortitude to keep on going. With gratitude of those simple things, I would prevail. I imagined putting any fears into that bag in a dumpster, and do away with that, which did not serve me. I would let go of the muck.

When I thought I was on my last rope, I kept pulling through it. I traced those areas within me holding me back, patterns I held onto. I unraveled the "could be's", "would "be's" and "should be's". I went back to my childhood. The ties my mother and I held were strained in ways, and somewhat taciturn. I needed to let go of expectations. Even though a healthful attachment was not something that was instilled in my earliest relationship, she was my mother. I needed to allow myself the honor in trusting my instincts without fear. I was courageous. I could see it. I could touch it. I could taste it. I could believe it. I owned this right. This was my gift to myself. This was my gift to Sierra. I had a choice each and every moment of every hour, and every day.

There were days I grew so damn tired. I wanted an escape. Someplace easier, where I didn't have to think of all that could happen, worried about the future. I shifted gears, giving more attention to myself, to my art, to my writing, to that which nourished me, that which I was passionate about.

There was so much beauty and power within each of us, and that which I could always turn to, myself. My daughter could walk. My daughter could run. Sometimes, we crawled for a while, before we walked. There was a time my daughter had hippo-therapy, I recalled a mom saying to me. "My! Look at her run!" I turned to see her son. He was no different than Sierra, nor any of us. Barely able to lift his head up, he got up from his wheel chair and with assistance, he assembled himself high up on that horse. He was ready to ride.

Another memory that touched me. I was at a local café. This little girl walked in with a skip in her step, uninhibited. It was as if she danced through the doorway. She had such a warm glow about her, and a contagious laugh. She sat in at the table behind us. There was a band there. She got up did a jig. I joined with her. We made small talk about what we were eating and drinking, what we enjoyed, etc. I was delighted by her innocence. She lit up the whole room. She was beautiful.

Another memory entered my mind. I had worked with a little boy on a Saturday program, as an art therapist. Behind the thick glasses, were these intelligent green eyes, light brown freckles upon his cheeks. His wheelchair faded into the background. He took a piece of colored tissue paper in one hand as I took another colored tissue paper in mine. His father's wish was that he would connect and interact more. I remained present, right in front of him. I was focused on him only, his endearing way. There was a rhythm that we had developed more together now as I entered his world without apprehension. As he wriggled his hands back and forth, I did too. He repeated this movement. There was a pattern performed, and I followed his lead. I turned my paper whimsically, at times in another direction just a little, watching for subtle cues in his eyes or his mannerisms and gestures. At once, my tissue paper met with his and it stuck! He turned to look at me. We connected! The look in his eyes was priceless. What an engaging smile! The two pieces of paper we each held in our hands served as a tool, a bridge to access something deeper. His father turned to me with tears in his eyes. His son made elated sounds. The joy I felt from both of them in my heart when I thought back to this time, was truly a gift.

This is Living

"This is living." It was what my father said most often at the dinner table, with an endearing smile. The simple things in life were most essential, as in the interaction between two, in appreciation of the present with love and compassion.

Upon entering my home, there was a doorway. I turned the key. It was golden. Although I sat in the same location, as I expressed my thoughts, my perspective shifted. I peered out the window pane. The branches appeared humble, in their vulnerabilities to fall. Each one had such grace, in their ability to move, and as a whole, it could weather the storms. The tree's energy held such wisdom. Reaching up and out from its rootedness in all its glory, from the soils that replenished its core, it was rich and whole and complete. Its embodiment held the nutrients for self-growth and renewal.

The sun shined through. The colors of life were bountiful.

To my love Sierra—

Shine your light. Express whatever it is you choose, and are able to, in the moment. Express who you are—your spirit, your love. Sweet child o' mine. Seek and discover what you may. It's your doorway. You have the key. Remember—You set the pace. Slow down as you need, or plummet right through. You will find that balance. There is no catching up. There is no grade. There is no failure. There is nothing else that serves you more, and nothing that has greater value, than life's simple abundance-You!

Sierra Brooke, Congratulations! You made it. You are Here.

Tomorrow

My daughter would soon be eight. Living beyond that seven-year cycle. What do they say about seven-year cycles? The seven-year cycles are a flow, a rhythm. It was not static. It changes. Perhaps, it is felt two years ahead, or three years later. It builds, peaks and wanes, like the tides. They have an evolutionary spiral that we all enter into, experience, and emerge through. There is a completion at the end of each one, and if we accept who we are and our greater purpose in life, we will fulfill our life's contract. It's our birthright. There is a divine way that the mind, body, and spirit work in harmony with the alignment of the universe. If we fight it, we pull against the very nature of our being, and what we bring as our gifts to the earth.

That infinite eight pattern was around the corner, for us to evolve. When it stood vertically, as in the number eight, there was a balance to calibrate within our own innate intelligence. There was more to unfold, as in life. When turned on its side, as horizontally the flow was more balanced. Sierra was experiencing her last year of seven. I wasn't too far off, approaching forty-eight. I had a little more than one more year in this cycle.

Changes were seen. Some were subtle, while others were greater. There was always a variability. Seasonally speaking, when winter had approached, Sierra would dip in terms of her auto-immunity and have pans flare-ups in early November. In the spring, she might dip a little again, then into healthier cycles, and blossom in the warmth of the summertime. Fall would come, again with changes in the air.

The cells within us had their own voice, their own power, and within them, we hoped for Sierra to come into her own. The stem cells, we prayed for them to give voice to each other, and circulate through those channels reminding the body, and brain of its innate intelligence.

Turning Eight

We had a family party to celebrate Sierra. We were hopeful that this year Sierra would emerge even more, through life in her own beautiful way, to grow healthfully. We found out from her school she would have a new teacher beginning in the summer. It was truly a blessing. Sierra had the opportunity to be part of the extended year program for children with special needs. During the summer, at drop off at the school, we were greeted with all smiles from Ms. Bryant. She was warm, bubbly, young and seemed very excited to work with Sierra and our family. She wrote in the log book almost every day, with smiley faces and with a tone of sincerity in truly wanting to help Sierra learn and grow. She was open to working with children in a more humane way. It was obvious to me how creative she was when we came to visit Sierra's classroom. On her doorway, covered in bright pink tissue paper, the words read, "My Very Sweet Class". This was evident of her kindness. She welcomed any ideas that could assist Sierra and brainstorming with us. Sierra had a young aide who was gentle and sweet. Sierra came home smiling, much of the time. In addition, her drivers who transported her to school each day, were very compassionate. They played music Sierra enjoyed, and gave us gifts on holidays, and on our birthdays.

Sierra's speech therapist since last year, remained working with her. She was very organized, and skilled in terms of speech techniques with an advanced understanding of the jaw mouth and tongue movements, grading techniques, and oral motor apraxia. Sierra continued to have speech three days a week, at an hour and a half a week. Every other week, she came into the classroom to assist the teacher and aide in terms of speech utilizing the augmentative device. I wasn't a big fan of this, only to support Sierra in lieu of removing frustration, if the staff was unable to understand her wants and needs. I preferred people actively listening to Sierra and help support her, even when the words were hard for her express. Ask Sierra questions. Then if necessary, to use the device. The interaction between them was more integral to learning, rather than pushing buttons to get one's needs met. Plus, the woman's voice on the device was monotone with little inflection. It was impersonal.

Her speech therapist continued to indicate that Sierra was making progress, yet slowly. She noted that Sierra had a fairly significant apraxia component. She wasn't non-verbal. She was verbal with a lot of challenges, as in repositioning areas within her body, to form and articulate the sounds with coordinated movements. To master the art of getting the words out concisely and consistently took a lot of effort. Sierra needed more speech within a broader context. It was essential she had a cohesive staff that utilized a collaborative approach between all disciplines. Greater integration between topics discussed during the day, would improve with emphasis on utilizing the body in sync with language, to better assimilate information.

Also, Sierra had developed a really nice relationship with another little girl in her class. She had been in her class a couple of years ago, when Sierra first started there. Alana was such a good friend to Sierra. The teachers remarked that she was a little bossy, in a sweet way. Such a wonderful quality. We could all use a little bossiness to get what we wanted. Sierra was very independent, confident and strong willed. It was a good match. She made gains that year in terms of social and emotional development.

Turning Nine

Sierra was turning nine. This birthday would be different. We had a party with friends of Sierra's. I invited Sierra's best buddy from her class, Alana. Also, I was fortunate to have met another mom at the Halloween parade that year. We had exchanged numbers. Since we lived a little farther from the school, it wasn't as accessible for us to attend many of the events there. It was school policy to refrain from having a roster for the parents to communicate with each other. It would have been helpful to connect with another mom in her class to share, learn, and grow from one another's experiences.

Sierra's best buddy came to celebrate Sierra's birthday. I was overjoyed. The mom I met with at the parade, arrived with her little girl. One of my dear friends from several years ago came with her sweet son, as well. It was in our backyard. Thankfully, it was a warm and sunny day. It was lovely. Sierra was happy and enjoying herself. It was a mermaid theme, which Sierra appreciated. She was elated, when she saw the table all set, and the pastel colored balloons. We had a magician, pizza and cake. Although it seemed like a typical event that happened in everyday life, to us it meant the world. I approached Alana, kneeled down a bit, and thanked her for being such a good friend to Sierra. She nodded her head, and pointed to her heart, to Sierra, and back to her heart, again. She articulated in so many words, that Sierra was a good friend to her. I had tears in my eyes. A memory I will always treasure. The nonverbal led to the expressive. It was springtime. Flowers were budding. A newness was in the air.

A Summation
of Colors

Sierra's love of books: From the beginning, when she was just one, she had turned the pages of several books. She spoke to me through these pictures. In songs, she conveyed to me her thoughts and her feelings—"Do you hear the people Sing" or "Four Hugs a Day." Yes, I hear you, Sierra "I'm listening". Also, I told her of the beauty within by placing my hand on her heart. "At least four hugs", I replied, enthusiastically.

One of Sierra's favorite songs, as a child was "Rainbow Connection", and another song, "True Colors". "Show them your smile. Don't be discouraged."

The spectrum exists within us all, in all our uniqueness. We each carry our own diversity of colors and variations in hues, or different shades. Our tone, pitch, and rhythm changes within we ourselves, over time, and therefore, in relation to one other. I aspired to live each day with an even, greater love. There was always room for self-growth. The heart was always open.

Each day, Sierra was living and telling us her story. In her wisdom and her grace, in her beautiful way, her voice was heard.

From my mouth to God's ears.
Thank you!

To all the families going through something
greater than you feel you can handle—
You are not alone.
You can do this.
Even in what seems like the darkest of times, there is a light.
There is a corner that you can turn.

You hold the key.
Let your inner wisdom be your guide.
You do not have to live in the shadows with fears of something
you see as unattainable and denied to you or your child.
You have a right to find it.
Whatever it is, be open.
It may change over the course of time.
There are answers.
There is hope.
There are prayers that are answered.

So—
Live the present.
Love the gifts that exist inside of you.
Love your child's gifts.
Allow the miracles that exist within, to shine through.

"With the greatest love and the most hope,
May you fulfill your dreams from here until, then."

This was the sentiment from my grandfather
Zachary Morris Greenwald.
He wrote this in my autobiography book,
when I was just eleven years of age.

…Time…
The words never fade.
The experience never lessens.
So, live the glory of today.

There is no momentary lapse of reason.
The answer to life is to,
Simply, live.

Bibliography

"The Interdisciplinary Council on Development and Learning." ICDL., accessed Mar 26, 2019, http://www.icdl.com/dir.

"What is Applied Behavior Analysis in Simple Terms?" ABA Degree Programs., accessed Mar 26, 2019, https://www.abadegreeprograms.net/faq/what-is-applied-behavior-analysis-in-simple-terms/.

"What is DIR®? - ICDL - DIR Floortime." The Interdisciplinary Council on Development and Learning., accessed Mar 26, 2019, http://www.icdl.com/dir.

"What is PROMPT Therapy?" The PROMPT Institute., accessed Mar 26, 2019, https://www.promptinstitute.com/page/FamiliesWIP.

63095554R00177

Made in the USA
Middletown, DE
25 August 2019